Traditional
Buildings
of India

TRADITIONAL
BUILDINGS
of INDIA

ILAY COOPER • BARRY DAWSON

With 220 illustrations, 92 in color

THAMES AND HUDSON

To my father, Bill Cooper, and remembering Tilak (Bilou) Sethi

Facing title page: Mural in Shekhawati district, Rajasthan, mid-nineteenth century
Title page: Decorated doorway, Kutch
Following pages: Rooftops in Lucknow, Uttar Pradesh

© 1998 Thames and Hudson Ltd, London

First published in the United States of America in 1998 by Thames and Hudson Inc., 500 Fifth Avenue, New York, New York 10110

Library of Congress Catalog Card Number 97-61642
ISBN 0-500-34161-3

Printed and bound in Italy

CONTENTS

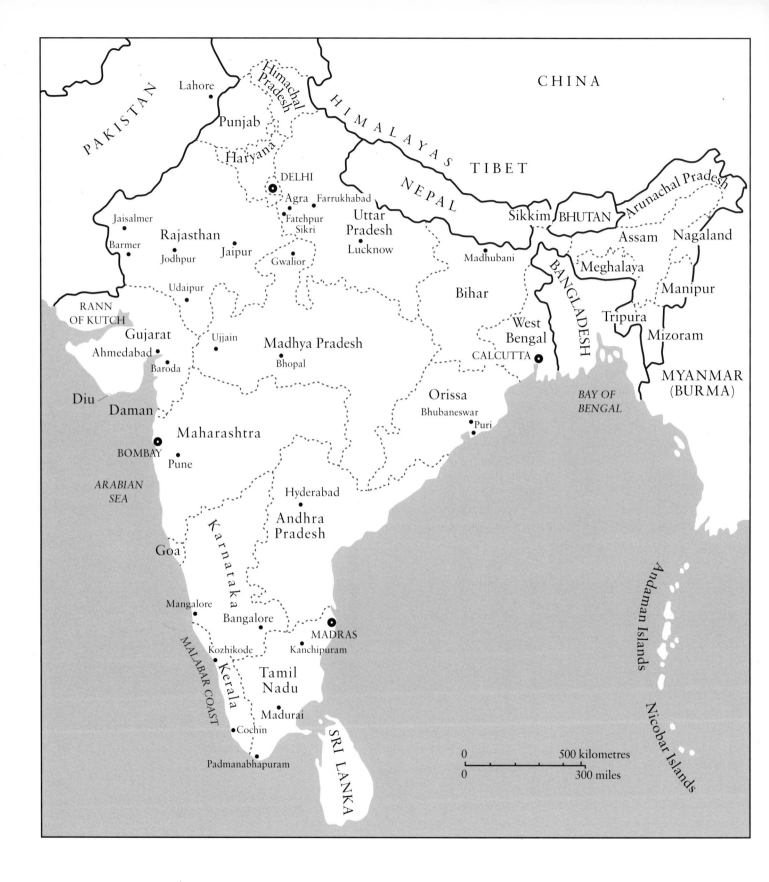

INTRODUCTION

THE INDIAN SUBCONTINENT is bounded to the west by the deserts of Baluchistan and neighbouring parts of Iran, to the north by the great mountain chains of the Hindu Kush and Himalayas, to the east by densely jungled hills. The Arabian Sea and Indian Ocean deter India's approach from the south. In this vast landmass a complex culture, recharged by periodic invasions from the West, developed into modern times as an individual entity. Around and within it a collection of minor cultures thrive.

Each community produces its own architectural forms and techniques, evolved to meet the challenges of a unique set of conditions. This book is divided geographically into regions which bring together similar climatic and social characteristics. This juxtaposes different solutions, drawing on a similar pool of resources, to an identical environment.

The climate is a primary influence on architectural form, not only in the challenges it poses to the builder but also in the materials it supports. Both timber and mineral hardpans require regular or seasonal rainfall: both are major building resources. India boasts a diverse range of climates. Dras, in Ladakh, is one of the coldest settlements on earth; during the hottest months, the temperature at Churu (Rajasthan) touches 50 degrees centigrade (122 degrees Fahrenheit). May is the height of summer, just before monsoon rains break the heat. The southwest monsoon influences most of the region, hitting Kerala's coast around 1 June, heading northwards to reach Delhi early in July. It comes as days of utter downpour to hills near the coast, as frequent high cloud and occasional rain to arid Rajasthan. Another, weaker monsoon from the southeast affects the peninsula's east coast during the winter months.

India's topography is equally diverse. To the north rises a wall comprising some of the highest mountains on earth, eternally snowbound. Elsewhere are lesser ranges – the Aravallis cutting across Rajasthan, the Vindhyas running east to west through Madhya Pradesh, and the Nilgiris in western Tamil Nadu as well as many others. The core of the peninsula is a great igneous plateau, the Deccan, with a scarp slope, the Western Ghats, plunging down to the coastal plain. The Eastern Ghats fall more gently to the eastern coast. There are huge, featureless alluvial plains, the rolling dunes of Rajasthan's desert. Under India's tricolour, too, come several groups of islands, including the Andamans and Nicobars to the east and the Lakshadweep group to the west.

Social customs leave an important mark on domestic architecture. There is a variety of requirements: some orthodox Muslims keep their womenfolk hidden, in *purdah* (literally, 'curtain'). This must be accomplished by a suitable house plan. For the poor this is difficult and often neglected. Hinduism inherited this tradition but imposes it more mildly. Hindu women are separated more by distance than invisibility. Since Independence there has been a weakening of the system amongst both communities. Most tribal communities are relaxed about the separation of the sexes. A house must be moulded to differing lifestyles. The merchant needs an office, the fisherman a place to store and work on his nets, the farmer a byre for his beasts against bad weather.

India's traditional architecture has evolved within these constraints: it may be defined as architecture without architects. Not that it dispenses with overall supervision, just that this is not in the hands of a sophisticated urban professional. Instead, it is vernacular in that it is the product of well tried local craftsmen raised in the use of local materials to confront local social and environmental conditions. If slow to change, it is not frozen but shows gradual evolution influenced by changing conditions and sometimes by knowledge of contemporary monumental forms and techniques. Its roots are ancient, planted by the earliest men to settle this land. Its branches grew out of their surroundings moulded by custom, adapting to diverse climates and topography. It brings together domestic building ranging from the the flimsy flood-plain village *jhonpri* (hutment), easily rebuilt and expected to perish yet again with the next severe monsoon flood, to the great urban *haveli* (mansion) built for some prosperous merchant by a local team of masons drawing on tradition and local resources.

Religious buildings and palaces are considered to be monumental, rather than traditional, architectural forms. They are products of a larger culture and are carefully planned by sophisticated men, often consciously competing with, or improving on the work of rivals. They draw on a wide selection of materials which may be brought from great distances. In this book they appear only when they reflect vernacular forms and techniques. Thus Kashmiri mosques and Keralan temples are included whilst Mughal mosques and northern Indian standard temples only feature in passing.

Despite formidable physical barriers defining the subcontinent migrating waves of mankind flowed in. Almost all came from the west, through Afghan mountain valleys or across arid Baluchistan, driving earlier settlers before them. They did not sweep in as rushing breakers in a storm, but advanced slowly, over decades, centuries, first eastwards, then to the south, conquering, destroying, intermingling. Coming as small tribes of hunters into inhospitable frontier lands, they were impelled by the presence of other advancing groups to find new pastures. Once past desert Baluchistan or mountainous Afghanistan a richer, more fertile world of forests and rivers opened before them. Prior to the age of settled agriculture, the inhabitants were nomadic, settlements temporary, poised to exploit nearby water, good hunting grounds and natural shelter. It was necessary that a site for settlement should yield tools, usually derived from some form of silica: flint, agate, jasper or quartz. That implied a rocky landscape, perhaps with caves to provide natural shelter. Their inhabitants painted their walls with the oldest remaining traces of Indian art. Central India is rich in decorated rock shelters.

The earliest human constructions must have resembled those of extant primitive societies, combining branches, leaves and stones to hold the elements at bay. From this developed a cylinder-and-cone dwelling, a circular hut supported by wooden posts, crowned by a conical thatched roof and walled with wattle and daub. This house-type, common to many Eurasian and African societies, appears in pre-Christian Indian art and remains common across the country.

Kachha *Architecture*

A tentative line may be drawn between two groups of building. Those constructed of short-lived materials – mud, sticks, grass – are defined as *kachha* (Hindi for unripe, raw, incomplete). They contrast with *pukka* (proper, ripe, cooked) structures made to last, using more tenacious material – worked stone or timber, burnt brick, lime plaster. Many combine several ingredients: Indian architects refer to them as 'semi-*pukka*' buildings. These are not specialized definitions but expressions in general usage.

Kachha architecture is truly vernacular, utilizing little-altered material from its immediate surroundings. The *kachha* house is generally built by members of the family, perhaps aided by their neighbours, following the tradition of the village. Each house varies little from those surrounding it, exploiting well tried technology and familiar resources. Mahatma Gandhi, during an Independence struggle as much against economic as political domination, continually promoted *swadeshi* (indigenous) products against smart *videshi* (foreign) rivals. He visualized free India as an independent nation of villages, each largely self-supporting in crafts and crops. For him the ideal house drew on material collected within a five-mile radius. Despite the conspicuous success of fifty years of industrialization, India remains essentially a rural, agricultural land. Although there is a constant flood of migrants into towns and cities it is in the countryside that the vast majority of people live. There is little will to promote traditional building: most villagers still aspire to escape it.

Rudofsky, in his *Architecture Without Architects*, points out that 'untutored builders fit their work in the environment and topography. They don't try to conquer nature.' India's wide range of environments and topography assures an equally wide range of response. The beauty of *kachha* architecture derives less from self-conscious decorative attempts than from pure, practical shapes produced by adapting local material as economically as possible to counter hostile environmental elements and to utilize beneficial ones. The Nagas of the northeast exploit versatile bamboo to combat a damp, mild climate, often creating handsome as well as functional structures. Rajasthanis in the western desert mould mud into glorious sculptural shapes which encourage draughts and are seldom threatened by rain. Himalayan folk half sink their rubble walls into the earth, blending into the topography for added protection from a bitter winter. Along the west coast roofs of thick paddy or coconut extend over large verandahs so that the inhabitants can work in shelter through the heavy monsoon. Meanwhile, peasants of the flood plains await the destruction of their flimsy homes with equanimity. Furniture is minimal, limited to a few mats, thin quilts and vessels for water and for cooking. These can be saved from the inundation and around them a new home will rise from the mud. Each rural builder adapts to environmental circumstances rather than fruitlessly confronting them. He works in the awareness that his construction often has a limited lifespan, mudwork and thatch decaying in a few years.

Most *kachha* architecture is decorated, usually in order to appease invisible spirits and demons, and to please locally worshipped deities. Whilst structural work is usually in male hands decoration is often the preserve of women. Embellishment varies, from a few handprints intended to fend off the 'evil eye' and textural designs in mud plaster to the lively figurative painting that covers Madhubani houses (Bihar). For its decoration, as for its fabric, rural housing develops a strictly local language. *Pukka* decoration, usually controlled by wealthy, sophisticated patrons, has responded to more cosmopolitan trends. While Mughal and British cultural power barely touched rural Indian buildings they left a heavy imprint on *pukka* architecture.

Towards Pukka *Architecture*

Solid housing is associated with sedentary life. As man turned to agriculture he settled, choosing a productive, well watered site. While most people put up *kachha* homes, the rich began building to last. Fertile land supported towns, towns concentrated wealth, and wealth produced monuments. The earliest settlements yet unearthed on the subcontinent are in Baluchistan (now in Pakistan), dating from around 5000 BC. The houses were still *kachha*, of sun-dried brick, probably thatched. Their inhabitants smelted copper, produced fine painted pottery and had already developed distant trading contacts. Recent excavations near Dera Ismail Khan (in Pakistan) revealed a town dating from the fourth millennium BC with a grid pattern of streets and a massive brick defensive wall. Already a concept of town-planning had emerged.

Colonization of rich alluvial lands in the Indus basin gave birth to the Harappan civilization. There, clearing forest, tending crops and protected from flood and foes by burnt-brick walls, India's first urban culture was developed. The heartland of this culture, and its greatest cities, Mohenjodaro and Harappa, lie in modern Pakistan, but it ranged east far into modern India, traced by remarkably uniform town plans, house forms and artefacts. Arranged along grid-plan streets were little brick courtyard houses. The central courtyard was to become a fundamental space in most urban housing. Amongst the Indian sites of greatest historical interest are Kalibangan (northern Rajasthan) and the erstwhile port of Lothal (Gujarat).

The Harappan civilization flourished from 2500 to 1750 BC before being swept aside by an unusually potent wave of invaders. Masters of horse and war chariot, the Aryans were nomadic. Urbanization was suspended.

The events which followed are loosely recorded in ancient Aryan texts, the Rig Veda (the oldest and principal sacred text of Hinduism) and its successors. Composed towards the close of the 'Vedic Age' (1500–600 BC), they describe conflict between Aryan warriors and an urban people, dark native worshippers of the *lingam* (phallus). These settled folk inhabited walled towns. Although Harappan-style houses continued to be constructed in such far-flung regions as Saurashtra (Gujarat) the concept of a permanent town lapsed for more than 500 years. The Aryan invasion gave rise to caste divisions, perpetuating a separation between conqueror and conquered. The Sanskrit word for caste, *varna*, also denotes colour. Shades of darkness differentiated (and still approximately differentiate) caste groupings.

Caste divides Hindu India into four major groups, each subdivided into a myriad of subcastes:

(1)   Brahmin, said to originate from the mouth of Brahma, the Creator: the priestly caste, aspiring to knowledge. Brahmins were responsible for sacred texts.

(2)   Kshatriya, coming from Brahma's arms: the Rajputs, including warriors and most of the princely rulers.

(3)   Vaishya, from the Creator's thighs: ranging from the important Bania (merchant) communities to various craftsmen and farmers. These three caste groupings descend from Aryan invaders.

(4)   Shudra, fashioned from Brahma's feet: embracing the rest of a diverse Hindu world and descended from indigenous people conquered by the Aryans. Traditionally 'untouchable', Shudras often have to perform unpleasant, 'unclean' jobs. Under India's constitution all are now officially equal.

The Aryans moved east until, at around the beginning of the first millennium BC, they, too, began to settle. Men began to question priestly authority, giving rise to revolutionary teachers such as Mahavir (founder of Jainism, an ascetic religion) and the Buddha. New cities that arose in eastern Uttar Pradesh and Bihar feature in the Hindu epics. This Gangetic civilization saw the dawn of India's historic period, recorded in scripts ancestral to modern Hindi. The Mauryan Empire was the most formidable regime of this culture, holding sway across much of the subcontinent under the enlightened rule of Ashoka (*c.* 269–232 BC).

Under the Mauryans fine stone masonry began to feature in the towns. Some elements, particularly pillars, resemble those of the Persian Achaemenid Empire, shattered by Alexander the Great's invasion of 326 BC. Perhaps craftsmen from a defunct empire were attracted to a rising one, leaving their mark on its architecture. The emperor Ashoka converted to Buddhism and the *stupa* form developed, a solid, flat-topped segment of a sphere to house a relic of the Lord Buddha. Constructed of brick, faced with stone and surrounded by a fence of railings, the *stupa* was increasingly enriched with fine sculpture. Amongst relief carvings are often illustrations of both urban and rural housing.

What survives of excavated, abandoned settlements is rarely more than wall footings and floors – plan but no elevation, as it were. The detritus of buildings may suggest their appearance but carved reliefs offer much more. Those on Buddhist *stupas* at Bharhut (Madhya Pradesh, first century BC) and later ones at Amaravati (Andhra Pradesh) and Sanchi (Madhya Pradesh) illustrate houses with rounded, tiled roofs as well as small thatched huts much like those of today.

Further clues to the appearance of early Indian traditional housing come from central Indian Buddhist, Hindu and even Jain monasteries and temples carved in living rock early in the Christian era. Many faithfully reproduce structural elements; basic to wooden architecture, most are merely decorative in carved rock. Massive beams recall wooden construction, while they are functionless, but rock shaped into pillars does help to sustain the ceiling. Fat and fluted, they must reflect a wooden prototype. Stone-carvers also reproduced *chaitya* arches similar to roofs shown in contemporary reliefs. The gable-end was wooden, the roof thatched, supported by curved timbers and purlins, rounded and rising to a central ridge. Reliefs show

Inscribed stele, Amaravati, showing stupa *complex.*

bricks and tiles but stone rarely features, save in foundations. Buildings portrayed largely in Buddhist art of the early medieval period are rarely flat-roofed. This is probably misleading, reflecting palatial rather than just smarter domestic housing. The standard town house may well have been flat-roofed, as it was in Harappan times and, over much of urban India, it still is. Certainly, some of the famous fifth-century Ajanta Cave paintings (Maharashtra) illustrate flat-roofed buildings.

Hindu scripture and tribal tradition intertwine with the rational structural considerations. Texts, the *shastras*, were written down by learned Brahmins as sacred justification for contemporary architectural practice, ensuring that priestly writ ran in this, as every other field. Aimed at the *sthpathi* (builder/architect), priest or householder, the *shastras* dictate auspicious orientation of buildings in relation to the cardinal points, to hills, running water, even the positioning of various plants. According to the *vastu shastra* each building plot contains a *vastu purusha*, a spiritual force, visualized as a male form crouched over the plot, head pointing northeast, feet southwest. The centre of this spirit, nucleus of the site, is a projected building's heart. In a temple this is marked by the *garbha griha* (sanctum). In a house it is occupied by the courtyard, the most sacred and private space. Variants of the *shastras* lay down local minutiae of construction related to different environmental demands.

A gulf separated this abstruse Sanskrit literature from illiterate builders on site. A *sutradhar* ('man with a measuring thread') still directs a team of *mistries* (masons) and labourers. Custom may have integrated shastric ideas into their practice but they are not familiar with the details. Vital in religious architecture, where a priest could interpret them, the texts were probably always distant from domestic reality, coinciding only when practical. A recent resurgence of Hinduism has re-established their authority. The *vastu shastra* in particular is currently heavily exploited by unscrupulous consultants to fleece a wealthy, but often credulous, Hindu business community.

Outside the field of these scriptures is a latent fear that buildings under construction are vulnerable to invasion by evil spirits, which either haunt it or render it inauspicious. India is peppered with houses abandoned because of their ghostly inhabitants. In the South such spirits are kept at bay by hanging a sometimes lifesize cloth doll from the scaffolding of a construction site.

Tribal communities have their own traditions and practices relating to the selection of building sites, orientation of buildings and rituals to accompany certain stages of construction. Some groups consider that to construct a house facing the rising sun (a temple's orientation) is arrogance. Others declare it wise. Although these traditions are constantly repeated in reality the tendency is for practicality to dominate: near a road, for instance, houses face the highway.

Northern India was still densely forested and timber remained the main architectural medium for all but religious buildings until Muslim times (thirteenth century onwards). From being an essentially monumental material, stone began to be used widely in temple building during Gupta times (*c.* 335–*c.* 500). The earliest stone temples were little more than cuboid chambers. In northern and central India it was during the eighth century that the *sikhara* (spire above the sanctuary) became

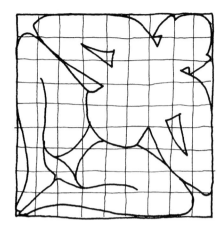

Diagram showing the plan of a house. According to the scriptures, each plot contains a vastu purusha, *a spiritual force represented by a male form, whose head points northeast and feet southwest. The centre of the form indicates the sacred centre of a building. This most private space in a house is the courtyard; in a temple, it is the* garbha griha, *or inner sanctum.*

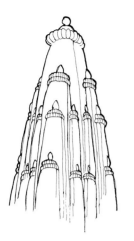

The sikhara, *or temple-tower, is built above the* garbha griha *or sanctuary. It became an important feature in the construction of Hindu temples from the eighth century onwards.*

The mandapa, *or hall for worshippers. The domed roof is built on ashlar courses converging from the supporting walls. These courses became the subject of ever more ornate decoration.*

an important feature of temple building. A northern temple traditionally consists of a *sikhara* (tower) over the *garbha griha* (sanctuary), which holds the principal deity, and a *mandapa* (hall for worshippers), which makes up the body of the temple. The *garbha griha* is generally surrounded by a corridor to permit devotees to circumambulate the deity, part of required ritual. In front of the shrine hangs a bell to draw the deity's attention to visitors.

From temples it is possible to see the general approach to architecture that was current in Hindu northern India. They were constructed with beams, horizontals and verticals constantly juxtaposed. Roofs of stone buildings were made up of large slabs of stone. *Sikhara* were constructed of flat stones rising from the outer shrine wall, gradually converging until the sides met. Even the domed ceiling of the crossing of a cruciform *mandapa* was achieved by a series of ashlar courses advancing to meet from supporting walls. There were occasional arches and even forms suggesting cusped arches. Increasingly, the temple became notable for decorative glory rather than basic form. Islamic domination of northern and central India helped to freeze temple evolution: there was little development after the twelfth century.

Dravidian temple architecture of the South began to develop an individual identity as early as the seventh century. Uninterrupted by the Islamic invasions, it was able to evolve into the eighteenth century. The characteristics of the style include a deeply moulded plinth, projecting eaves surrounded by a parapet, and walls divided by pairs of pilasters into alternately projecting and recessed bays. The major southern schools are Chola (ninth to thirteenth century, Tamil Nadu), Hoysala (twelfth and thirteenth century, Karnataka) and Vijaynagar (fourteenth to sixteenth century). The most characteristic southern temples are those of Tamil Nadu, as seen at Madurai, Tiruchirapalli and Rameshwaram, with huge *gopura* (gateways) and pillared halls. Local temple styles developed. Some were merely variants on the two major schools. Others, as in Bengal, Himachal Pradesh and Kerala, were truly vernacular.

Buddhism dominated Indian society followed by Hinduism until the close of the twelfth century. Islam arrived in the South perhaps as early as the seventh century. It came peacefully, with traders, and adopted vernacular models for its mosques. It took the North by conquest, arriving in the eighth century, when Syrian Arabs owing allegiance to the Ommayid Empire seized Sind (Pakistan). Four centuries later Afghan Muslim invaders controlled much of northern India.

The Delhi Sultanate, founded in 1193, gave birth to an Indo-Islamic style which transformed Indian architecture. Domes and pointed arches constructed of voussoirs (wedge-shaped bricks or stones used to create a vault or arch), quite alien to indigenous forms, spread with the Islamic faith. It was not until Muslim rule was well established that worked stone was widely used in secular building.

Significant amongst early Islamic buildings were tombs. Hinduism does not magnify the termination of earthly life. It sees the soul as bound into an eternal circuit of reincarnations. Cremation is usual and memorials, if any, were modest. By the sixteenth century Muslim tombs had inspired wealthy Hindus to erect *chhatris* (domes) over cremation sites.

One early Sultanate offshoot established itself at Gaur (Bengal). Later, as Delhi rule weakened, another dynasty, the Bahmani, took over Gulbarga (now Karnataka). By the close of the fourteenth century the governors of Gujarat, Malwa (Madhya Pradesh) and Jaunpur (Uttar Pradesh) were all independent rulers developing their own interpretation of Islamic architecture. Variable in tolerance, these regimes spelled disaster for Hindu religious architecture. The threat continued until the death of Emperor Aurangzeb in 1707. Throughout this almost uncontested Muslim domination of north and central India, a number of wise rulers, either from political acuity or personal inclination, maintained positive policies of tolerance.

Founded by an Uzbek warlord, the Mughal dynasty (which flourished 1526–1712) synthesized a distinctive Indo-Islamic architectural tradition. It was responsible for some of India's finest monuments, introducing forms which, in turn, were indelibly to mark traditional architecture. The emperor Akbar (ruled 1556–1605), in common with the Sultans of Gujarat (whom he overthrew), integrated Hindu trabeate forms into his buildings. But the tomb he built in Delhi for his father, Humayun, followed Islamic domed and arched tradition. His son, Jahangir (ruled 1605–27), continued this Hindu-Islamic synthesis, adding the *bangla*, an arched sloping roof copied from Bengali brick-built temples and *kachha* hutments, to Mughal forms. Shah Jahan (ruled 1628–58), orthodox in faith and deeply interested in architecture, deflected building away from Hindu towards Persian Islamic models already popular in India. Pure lines, arches and domes, the hallmarks of fine Islamic construction, reached their zenith under his rule.

From the early eighteenth century to its demise in 1858 the Mughal empire declined. Although rapidly decaying, the forms which had come to typify the empire – increasingly bulbous domes, cusped, pointed and shouldered arches, *bangla* roofs – represented its strength and genius: they were picked up by rising powers. Punjabi Sikh and Rajasthani Rajput rulers developed them for their palaces, memorials and temples. The inspiration flowed into more modest religious and domestic building. Mughal structural elements and decoration are wholly integrated into much modern traditional architecture.

It is hard to know how much *haveli* (mansion) layout was Mughal-inspired since its early ancestry is obscure. Mughal legislation decreed that wealth and property should revert to the imperial treasury on its owner's demise. This discouraged wealthy courtiers from magnificent urban building but they certainly adopted *haveli* form. Descriptions of Delhi *havelis* in the mid-seventeenth century indicate that many, though handsome, were built of ephemeral mud brick. A nobleman might conceal some goods with which to endow his heirs but he could not hide his residence.

It is impossible to accept Islamic influences on Indian traditional architecture and ignore those of Europe. European colonial settlement, albeit on a small scale, preceded the Mughal empire's foundation. Vasco da Gama arrived on India's coast in 1498. In 1510, fifteen years before Babur, first Mughal emperor, took Delhi, the Portuguese made Goa their centre of Indian operations. They set up other coastal enclaves including Daman (north of Bombay) and Diu (an island off the Gujarat coast), holding them until evicted by Indian troops in 1961. In Mughal times, these

Jali, or carved latticework screen. *Allowing the passage of air and light in a hot climate, the distinctive decorative patterns show Mughal origins. Features of Islamic architecture became integrated with other indigenous forms in northern India.*

were vital centres for European Catholic influence. Jesuits featured importantly at the courts of Akbar and Jahangir. The products of European art and ingenuity they bore impressed their hosts more than the faith they attempted to purvey.

Naturally, the first European buildings in India were those of the Portuguese, the churches, houses and palaces of their coastal towns. In contrast with all other cultural and martial invasions the Europeans penetrated India's interior from the coast, either from the ports where they set up factories or from the enclaves they held. Other Europeans followed, drawn by tales of fabulous wealth. Apart from the Portuguese there were territories held by the French, the Dutch and even the Danes. From the late eighteenth century onwards the British dominated and Calcutta was the prime architectural influence on populous northern India.

With Calcutta as its capital the British regime spread over the north, always seeking a firm, stable frontier. The rise of British power in India was accompanied by the foundation and mushrooming of three British-founded ports. Each became an important centre of local power, each displayed European planning, secular and religious architecture to a receptive audience. These cities, Madras in the South, Bombay in the West and Calcutta, the new capital, in the East, had a profound effect on neighbouring visions of building. European forms soon became fashionable. They did not always come directly from the new paramount power. The rulers of Oudh (Uttar Pradesh) in their capital, Lucknow, were much influenced by a Frenchman, Claude Martin, who settled there and built several palatial houses in Palladian style. Martin died in 1800 by which time European architectural forms were well established in local urban building.

Much of the population was glad to welcome the new regime after a century of instability. Even at the height of British power forty per cent of the country was held by native princes. By 1818 most of these rulers had ratified treaties accepting British paramountcy. There followed the longest period of internal peace in the known history of India, interrupted only by the Mutiny of 1857 and ended by the Partition of 1947. As a result, the nineteenth century was an era of unparalleled prosperity for mercantile India. Merchant wealth was poured into handsome traditional building.

In Calcutta and other major British centres colonial domestic and administrative building turned to the Graeco-Roman classical tradition. India was once again confronted with imperial grandeur. The wealthy were impressed and north Indian *haveli* stucco work soon reflected European classical forms. Anglo-Indian buildings appeared throughout the country as government offices, schools, colleges and the ubiquitous 'bungalow'. This last was another adaptation of Bengali traditional housing, not in its arched roof but its covered verandah, often on all four sides. It became the model for British houses in India, replacing a private courtyard with a semi-public verandah.

Outside influence often overwhelmed traditional form. In the South, particularly in Kerala, long-established Christian communities followed vernacular temple form for their churches. As Portuguese enclaves developed the local Christians used their Iberian style as a model. Similarly, Keralan Muslims initially constructed mosques on the lines of wooden temples but later turned to Mughal models for inspiration.

The main patrons of large-scale traditional domestic architecture in the nineteenth and twentieth centuries were rich merchants. Lockwood Kipling (Rudyard's father), writing in 1886, remarked:

> the trading and money-lending classes alone are now seen to be the support of the mistry, or native builder and architect. In Gujarat, Kattiawar [western Gujarat], Rajputana [Rajasthan], Northern India and the Punjab this individual is the sole depository and trustee of the principles and traditions which form the roots of Indian art.

Under British rule there was relative peace and stability. A classic colonial trade pattern developed. Raw materials such as cotton and jute poured out of the country and British-manufactured goods returned. The native textile industry so vital to India's economy was swept away, but traders flourished. They soon realized that under the new regime they need not fear to display affluence. So they built – and on a grand scale. Traders, in common with other caste Hindus, looked down on the foreigners but admired their achievements and their inventiveness. European features began to appear in their houses. Often a special European room was added, in which foreign or anglicized guests could be entertained. Here the furnishing was Western-influenced, and included chandeliers, glass lamps, glass paintings, coloured glass windows and other motifs then fashionable in the West. But the merchants were inherently conservative. There was no question of adapting to an alien house form quite unsuited to their normal life pattern.

Traditional urban domestic architecture harmonizes with the local climate. In the plains, where temperatures are extreme, walls and flat roofs are often massive for purposes of insulation. Broad *chhajjas* (eaves) project over external and courtyard walls, shading them from the sun, and deflecting monsoon downpours from the fabric of the building. Windows are plentiful but unglazed to allow efficient ventilation, closed instead by wooden shutters. Certain bedrooms are partly or wholly open to the sky, cooling rapidly after the sun has set. But the lung and the light of the whole structure is the courtyard, protected by the surrounding building from direct sunlight, the rooms and *dalans* with their arched entrances all opening onto it. Often roofs and terraces drain into a tank beneath the courtyard, providing the household with a reservoir of sweet rainwater. François Bernier, writing in north India during the 1660s, describes the priorities in urban building:

> In these hot countries a house is considered beautiful if it be capacious, and if the situation be airy and exposed on all sides to the wind, especially to the northern breeze. A good house has its courtyards, garden, trees, basins of water, small jets d'eau in the hall or at the entrance and handsome subterranean appartements which are provided with large fans… no handsome dwelling is ever seen without terraces on which the family may sleep during the night.

Three methods were developed to keep a large urban *haveli* cool during the heat of summer. A *teh khana*, the subterranean apartment Bernier describes, is sunk well

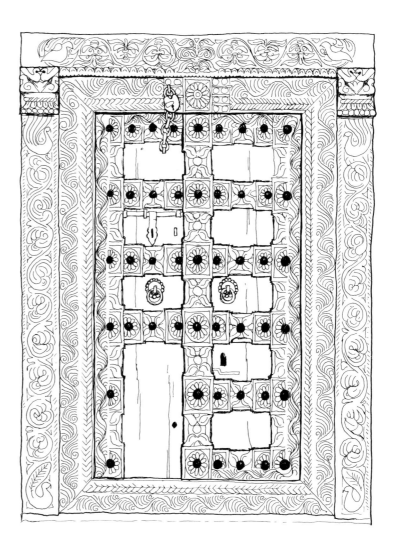

Ornate carving of wooden doors and doorways characterizes northern Indian architectural styles. Often brass or other metals add to the decorative effect, as well as serving practical functions of security. A small inset door provides everyday access.

into the earth, retaining a temperature little affected by external fluctuation. Screens made from dried *khus* grass roots were hung in front of window and door openings and frequently wetted. The draught passing through these wet screens was not only cooled; it was also scented by the grass. A third feature was the *punkah* (fan), so familiar to the British colonials. Fanny Parks was struck by it in the 1820s:

> The first sight of a pankha is a novelty to a griffin [new arrival in India]. It is a monstrous fan, a wooden frame covered with cloth, some ten, twenty, thirty or more feet long, suspended from the ceiling of a room, and moved to and fro by a man outside by means of a rope and pullies, and a hole in the wall through which the rope passes; the invention is a native one; they are the greatest luxuries, and are also handsome, some being painted and gilt...

After Independence alien house forms became more common, blossoming in city suburbs. Concrete and steel tempted with their very modernity, and with the shapes and spaces they could create. They might have to be brought long distances but rail and road traffic had revolutionized transport. So the Indian elite followed a trend engendered in the USA, building concrete villas, thin-roofed, generously glazed, ignoring old-fashioned traditional features. The resultant building was exposed to the full heat of the sun, for which the design made no allowance. Heavy curtains are required to shield large areas of glass from summer glare. The resulting gloom calls for artificial light in daytime. Thin concrete roasts gently in the rising sun, demanding the use of fans and cooling systems. Not only are such houses characterless, and often ugly; they encourage profligate waste of energy. With frequent power cuts, the glory of such a place is soon compromised.

Since the mid-1970s the enormity of the folly involved in building concrete-and-steel suburban houses has finally started to be recognized. India, prospering as a free state, is regaining that self-confidence so effectively destroyed by colonial rule. Some of the wealthy, dissatisfied with the sort of housing currently available, have started patronizing architects who specialize in vernacular designs. So the sophisticated urban architect is finally learning to exploit traditional materials, forms and techniques. Their homes prove cheaper not only in the initial outlay but also in running cost. There are a number of such Indian architects: their doyen is Laurie Baker, a Keralan by conviction rather than birth. With considerable success, he has relaunched the traditional building onto Kerala's housing market. Perhaps Indian urban architecture is emerging from a modernist concrete tunnel to turn again towards a rich vernacular vocabulary of materials and forms? As city-dwellers still look westwards for inspiration so rural folk turn towards the city. If a fashion for the traditional is established amongst the urban rich it will filter down to rural folk and they will cease to yearn for a concrete cube.

CHAPTER ONE

MATERIALS AND CONSTRUCTION TECHNIQUES

TRADITIONAL ARCHITECTURE develops its individuality by tapping nearby resources and exploiting them to confront problems posed by a local environment. Heavy rainfall calls for a steeply pitched waterproof roof to carry water clear of the living area, whilst extended eaves protect the wall fabric from water damage. If rain is seasonal the roof structure must also function efficiently in the dry season. When this is warm a large, high roof space continuous with the living area is practical. When cool, a ceiling confining the room space is useful, also providing a storage attic. The roof material has to be able to confront damp. Thick thatch is commonly used, easily available in agricultural areas, drawn from straw left after harvesting the staple grain crop. This is often rice, since the crop requires heavy rainfall. Thick thatch produces not only a waterproof roof but also a well insulated one. Every material has negative features, however, and thatch tends to house a rich fauna, including parasites, rodents and birds, all looking to the human inhabitants for sustenance. Stone is rarely available in the rich alluvial plains but fine clays are characteristic of riverine soils. Man soon learned to put this to use for plaster, sun-dried brick and later, burnt brick and tile.

Strong prevailing winds engender an architectural response that usually results in lower, flatter buildings offering less resistance and thus less prone to damage. Temperature extremes call for thick insulating walls and roofs to maintain a comfortable internal environment. When such extremes occur on river plains away from the threat of frequent flooding or in hot desert they are combatted by massive mud walls and roofs. Some regions suffer regular calamities. The response to coastal cyclones and regular inundation along the flood plains is to use cheap, light materials so that the building, inevitably destroyed, is easily rebuilt. Earthquake may be counteracted by integrating tensile timber elements into an otherwise rigid wall.

Each building material displays different physical characteristics. Parts of the structure require rigid strength to support the dead weight of the roof and walls. This is best achieved with stone or lime-mortared brickwork. Others must be tensile to respond to varying loads produced by wind or the movement of people within the building. Here, wood and bamboo are ideal.

If environment decides the range of suitable materials, together they dictate form. India's vast and variable landmass is diverse in geology and climate. This provides her builders with a wealth of mineral and plant material to satisfy their demands.

Recent archaeological exploration has revealed more of the history of building. Early manmade brushwood shelters inspired more ambitious use of wood, coupled with thatch and hide. Wattle (woven branches) followed. Mud was plastered over it, reducing heat-loss and draught, and increasing privacy. The prototype wattle-and-daub thatched hut was born and has flourished, virtually unaltered, into modern

A house in South Bengal nearing completion. The uprights are set in a plinth of mud and rubble. Mud walls are then constructed in courses of about 450 mm, showing darker when fresher. The bamboo roof structure is lashed onto the uprights, ready for paddy thatch.

India. The ephemeral nature of the materials has meant that they are rarely recovered in archaeological digs so it is not known when wattle-and-daub first appeared in India. The earliest recorded structure of this kind was unearthed in central India and dated from the third millennium BC, but the type is far older than that.

Malleable when wet, rigid when dry, the potential of mud as a building material must have been apparent at an early stage of human development. It remains a primary building material in rural India, its versatility only beginning to be appreciated by formal architects. Usually wet mud is used directly, mixed with cow dung, and perhaps given more body by adding chopped straw, gravel or stone. A wall is built up in courses about a foot high, each left to dry until it can bear the next. This is the most common method of mud building. The Santal tribe of Orissa and Bihar use a variant, souring earth by the addition of vegetable waste and leaving it to mature. The decaying waste produces tannic acid and other organic colloids, greatly improving the mud's plasticity. It is then cut into slices to use as building blocks. In Ladakh (Jammu and Kashmir), where rainfall is very low, another form of mud construction involves the use of wood shuttering within which a course of mud rich in river gravel is beaten down. When a course is dry the shuttering is raised, and the process repeated. The result is a compact, well consolidated wall. (Today this technique is rarely used, Ladakhis preferring to manufacture their own sun-dried brick on site.) Similarly, the leatherworkers of the Kohlapur region (Maharashtra) make building blocks by pounding a mixture of mud and pebbles into large square moulds, then drying them in the sun.

Mud provides the formative matrix for walls of rounded river boulders in the Himalayan foothills and of rough stone rubble masonry over much of the subcontinent, sometimes constituting most of the fabric's mass. Mud provided the earliest form of mortar and is still in use for brick and ashlar work. Protected from excessive contact with water, well consolidated clay is remarkably tenacious, surviving in foundations for several thousand years. When combined with cow-dung and textured or burnished, it provides a very handsome, durable plaster finish for walls and floors, not only of village huts but also, until recently, urban mansions. Mud mixed with grass, laid on birch bark, was the usual material used for pitched roofing in Kashmir. It often produced a veritable rooftop garden of plants.

Clay varies in colour with local geology, from buff in the alluvial plain to lateritic red along the peninsular coast. The colour is occasionally altered by some additive, such as ash which the Santals of Orissa and Bengal mix in to produce a cement grey. Some tribal folk cover wall surfaces, particularly that of the verandah, with votive figurative work or blocks of natural colour, ochres or lime. Mud plastering is usually the women's task and they tend to paint or work a range of textural designs into the surface. These usually have a ritual significance. Handprints, often in light earth colours, deflect the 'evil eye' and discourage destructive spirits. Depictions of certain deities convey blessings on the house. Some, like Ganesh, are positioned over the entrance, blessing each who enters. Others are painted as part of some ritual. Lakshmi, Goddess of Fortune, is drawn at Diwali, her autumnal festival, to be the focus of *puja* (worship). Some decoration imparts good fortune on crops or hunting. Some records the rank or achievements of the inhabitant.

Below left:
Constructing the wall of a Rajasthani jhonpri *or hut. This is first set out flat on the ground. Strengthening ribs are set in pairs on either side of the wall and stitched together through the fabric with twine. The wall is set upright as a cylinder, then coated with a mud-and-dung plaster.*

Middle:
Wall of flat stone fragments, Arki, Bihar. Since these are not exactly plane the builder fits in small irregular stones to keep his courses level. This is particularly important when little or no mortar is used.

Right:
Laterite blocks. Along the coasts of tropical India where there is heavy seasonal rainfall, an iron-rich hardpan, the product of leeching, collects beneath the surface. This sets hard when exposed to air. Dug and shaped, it is a primary building material.

23

Sun-dried mud brick appeared in the Indian subcontinent around 5000 BC: settlements from that period have been found in Baluchistan (Pakistan). The new medium was drifting in with new peoples from the west. Mud brick was the principal material employed in the rise of the Indus culture (now generally known as the Harappan civilization, from Harappa in Pakistani Punjab, one of its major cities) which flourished from 2500 to 1750 BC, India's first civilization. This culture spread from the Indus Valley as far as western Uttar Pradesh and eastern Gujarat. Mud brick remains a vital element in the vocabulary of India's vernacular architecture. Fashioned in wooden moulds from local clays that vary greatly in quality, bricks are simply laid out in the sun and turned until thoroughly dry.

The Harappan civilization was built on the technology for firing these bricks. Unlike sundried mud, the terracotta – fired clay – withstands the prolonged direct contact with water inevitable for any settlement in an alluvial flood plain. The Indus Valley, along which the civilization emerged, owes its fertility in part to annual flooding. Harappan towns are characterized by ramparts of burnt brick, raised as much for protection from monsoon inundation as from hostile armies. Permanent settlements built with this material allowed the inhabitants to exploit the surrounding flood plain's agricultural potential, generating sufficient wealth to finance the subcontinent's earliest surviving monuments – including palaces, granaries, water tanks and even the great dock at Lothal (Gujarat). In Harappan domestic architecture, terracotta provided floor tiling, drainage channels and brickwork for bathroom walls. The rest of the house was of sun-dried brick.

A Rajasthani mural shows a gharat *in action. A circular trench is filled with coarse lime, brick fragments and sand. A buffalo pulls a heavy stone wheel along the trench, its axle fixed at the centre of the circle, grinding the lime, brick and sand to mortar. One man is shown (bottom left) carrying mortar up to the builders. The mural painters were also the builders – their names are written at the top.*

The standardized British brick was adopted towards the end of the nineteenth century. Soon it was locally made throughout the country, replacing the native biscuit-like model. Here, the mould bears swastikas, symbolizing the Lord of Beginnings, Ganesh.

Coloured ceramic tilework as a decorative form was introduced to India by the Muslims. Generally the designs were geometric.

Burnt brick disappeared with the Harappans. It did not reappear until the fifth century BC. Since the Mauryan Empire (321–185 BC), however, it has been a primary building medium in the populous Indian plains. In the Punjab and the Ganges Basin, where deposits of alluvial clay cover the bedrock, it formed the fabric for generations of Buddhist, Hindu, Muslim and British monuments, and much of the more permanent domestic architecture. The Mughal emperor Akbar (ruled 1556–1605) used brick to build the fort and the city walls of Lahore (now in Pakistan) and around them rose brick tombs, caravanserais, mosques, palaces, *havelis* (mansions) and brick-paved streets of little houses. Builders and architects enhanced brickwork with colour or pattern. Muslim architects turned to Persian custom and faced brickwork with colourful tiles. Although primarily used to decorate monumental architecture, in the sixteenth century the coloured tile was taken up less widely for housing, tombs and wells. In the mid-nineteenth century the British introduced colourful square ceramic tiles. Locally produced, these achieved a vogue in domestic housing between 1910 and 1940 for decorating interiors and facades. In Bengal bricks and tiles were moulded and cut with decorative or figurative patterns.

Brickwork itself is often arranged decoratively to break the austerity of a wall. Courses of bricks set on edge, diagonally or with their corners projecting enliven the surface. They are also laid to make ventilating *jalis* (latticework screens), either simply by stepping the bricks, setting them on edge, with their axes at right angles to that of the wall, to produce square gaps, or placing them in alternate horizontal and diagonal courses, producing a series of triangular apertures in the brickwork.

The preferred brick size fluctuated. Those of the Harappan civilization were made in a 4:2:1 proportion, 10 by 5 by 2½ inches being common. In recent centuries, the little, biscuit-like indigenous 'Lakhauri' brick was preferred. The name may have derived either from the city of Lahore or from the numbers of these bricks (one 'lakh' is 100,000) required to build anything. There could be considerable variation in brick size from top to bottom of the wall, those of the lower courses being longer and broader.

The British introduced a standard 9 by 4½ by 3 inch brick, imposed on England by a statute of Charles I in 1625. Soon this was in use for all major government construction in India. By the close of the nineteenth century it was the established model for vernacular as for monumental building. British innovations, including steel girders, cement and corrugated iron, were developed for Indian usage and propagated by new educational establishments, especially Thomason Civil Engineering College at Rurki (Uttar Pradesh). Traditional Indian building technology was studied, too, and regularly published in 'Professional Papers on Indian Engineering', manuals for imperial engineers, dealing with native materials and usage as well as introducing European methods. Papers deal with such subjects as the construction of plaster *jalis*, traditional Punjabi flat-roof construction, the manner of producing *chunam*, a finely burnished stucco widely used in the best Indian building, and traditional mural-painting techniques.

The plains of India are dotted with the rickety metal chimneys of trench kilns. Dried bricks interspersed with fuel (such as brushwood, cow dung or paddy straw) are placed in a continuous trench along which fire travels. The burnt bricks it leaves

Left:
A Rajasthani open brick-kiln. Sun-dried bricks are built into a dome, alternating with layers of brushwood. The fuel is lit and the whole structure – the 'clamp' – is sealed with earth and left to burn, then to cool. A watchman is housed nearby to prevent bricks from being taken.

Below left:
Dome-like storage huts, Vishnupur, West Bengal. Standing some ten feet high, they are built from mud-plastered standard brick.

Right:
'Roman' tiles made by bisecting thrown clay cylinders. Tiles vary considerably in form in different parts of the country: some are moulded, some thrown.

Below right:
A potter throws clay cylinders which will be sun dried, then longitudinally bisected, each yielding a pair of 'Roman' tiles ready for firing. Beside the potter is brushwood for the kiln. Madhubani, Bihar.

behind are replaced by more dried bricks and more fuel. Thus firing can continue uninterrupted. More primitive are open clamp kilns, varying in shape from mounds in Rajasthan to low cylinders or stepped ziggurats in Andhra Pradesh. These consist entirely of dried bricks and fuel, often straw or brushwood. The whole is covered with earth, to be demolished when firing is completed.

Burnt brick used in combination with lime plaster allowed the construction of deep wells, which enabled trading caravans to cross the Rajasthan desert. A cylindrical masonry tower was built, then undermined so that it sank down the shaft as it was dug, consolidating its sides. Today, tubular cement pipe sections are used.

Tile competes with thatch as the principal material for pitched roofing throughout India. Amongst several forms of locally made terracotta tile, most common is the 'Roman' type, semicircular in cross-section. Wheel-thrown by local potters as a bottomless wide-necked bottle, it is cut in two lengthways before firing. Wheel-thrown tiles of this sort, giving roofs a corrugated look, are common from China to South America. A shorter, flatter tile is made over a wooden mould. Another more or less rectangular, flat tile has turned up lateral edges. All of these, tied to the purlins, are laid in courses alternately face up or face down, running down the pitch of the roof. Each tile tapers, fitting snugly under the next upslope, making the roof water-tight. Bamboo splits are sometimes lashed across the roof slope to secure the tiles. In Andhra Pradesh and Tamil Nadu the neck of the 'bottle' thrown to make a 'Roman' tile is severed before the cylinder is cut longitudinally in two. These necks, gripped by two bamboo splits running along the eave, are arranged along the bottom edge of the roof, adjoining the down-curving courses, helping to hold them in place.

In many parts of India *deshi* (country-made) tiles have given way to 'Mangalori' ('from Mangalore', in Karnataka) or *firenghi* (foreign, i.e. European) factory-made moulded tiles. More resilient and lighter, these require a less bulky roof structure, thus less timber. Even where Mangalori tiles are used, ridge tiles are usually still locally produced or are rendered redundant by imaginative use of ordinary tiles. Standard semi-circular ones are used in parts of central India, laid along the ridge in five rows. The uppermost row, with both straight edges set in corresponding rows, is set curve upwards, either edge set in a course laid curve downwards. These are supported likewise by courses interlocking with those running down the pitch. In the South, including in Tamil Nadu, short, moulded *deshi* tiles are arranged at an angle along the ridge like a fallen row of dominoes. This system is inefficient, often needing a matrix of cement or plaster to seal inherent leaks. In parts of north central India, including Chanderi (Madhya Pradesh), the ridge of stone-slate roofs is protected by overlapping potsherds (fragments of earthenware).

Through most of the country the use of burnt brick and tile in domestic architecture is ancient. In Kerala their introduction is traditionally credited to early Europeans – namely Portuguese or Dutch. In fact here, too, they had already long been known. To protect their factories and goods European traders petitioned local rulers for the right to tile their roofs. In gaining sanction they helped break a royal monopoly. For centuries after tiles were first adopted, tiled roofs were the prerogative of royal and temple architecture. Only in the mid-nineteenth century

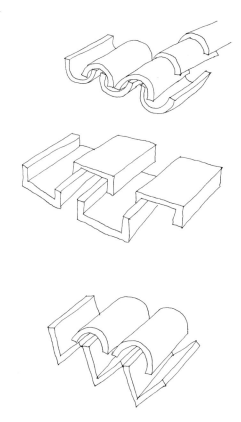

Top:
Simple half-cylinder 'Roman' tiles overlap in courses down the slope of the roof.

Middle:
Moulded rectangular tiles are widely used, either exclusively, as here, or in conjunction with 'Roman' tiles, the latter forming the upper element.

Bottom:
V-shaped moulded tiles, although less common, are seen in some regions, usually in combination with 'Roman' ones.

Drainpipes are achieved with cylindrical elements similar to those destined for tiles. These are fitted together snugly and set completely or partially into the fabric of the wall.

were tiles permitted for ordinary housing to reduce fire risk. Previously, paddy and coconut thatch, both inflammable, were the main roofing media.

Terracotta provides tiles for paving, as well as for bridging the gap between neighbouring joists to support a floor or flat roof of mortar or mud. Where stone is easily worked it usurps these roles. Traditional drainpipes are constructed by fitting a series of wheel-thrown, taper-ended terracotta sections into each other.

Another ingenious use of terracotta allows for the insulation of a flat roof without imposing too much weight. Inverted water pots are set close together all over the surface above the joists and a wet mortar mixture poured around and over them. The resulting roof consists mainly of hollow pots, the air in them insulating the roof whilst keeping its mass relatively low. In the 1870s my great-grandfather adapted this method for his quarters in Lucknow, having water-pots arranged all over its thin flat roof. A similar technique is used to increase the insulating properties of the ceilings of *teh khane* (cool basement rooms). Here, pots or short, drainpipe-like lengths are set on end in the mortar. Until recently it was common to base wooden uprights in terracotta pots to protect them against white ants which devour the timber.

Stone may only be used as a primary material if it can be easily worked or if natural fragments lend themselves to building. Some stones have clear bedding planes, cleaving to yield flat slabs ideal for structural elements and roof slates. Best are the sandstones quarried around the eastern borders of Rajasthan. Often bearing fossil ripple-marks, these split into *patta* (planks) up to 15 feet long making ideal lintels, door and window surrounds, joists or cantilevered steps. In widespread use thanks to modern transport, these *patta* have transformed traditional architecture in parts of Rajasthan. A dearth of timber for joists resulted in small rooms with a vaulted ceiling of rubble and lime mortar. This was built up on a mud mould supported by brushwood laid over temporary timber scaffolding set in the walls. *Patta* have rendered such ceilings defunct. The hill areas of Kumaon and Garhwal (Uttar Pradesh), Himachal Pradesh and Jammu are rich in less spectacular slates.

Standard North Indian *pukka* architecture requires stone for paving, steps, *chhajja* (sun-shading eaves), carved pilasters and above all for multitudes of *toda* (brackets) to support projecting stone floors, roofs and connecting walkways. Grey, naturally cleaving Kota stone (from Rajasthan) is used for paving, *jharokhas* (closed balconies) and steps as well as local slates and structural elements. Today, it is available throughout India.

Cutting and shaping hard stone is labour-intensive, which limits its use to ambitious domestic or monumental building. Working the red sandstone of western Uttar Pradesh and Rajasthan, local masons turn out ashlar, brackets, door and window surrounds, coping and *jali* (latticework). In a hot climate the lattice screen is a perfect replacement for glazed windows. On the principal of the lace curtain it protects privacy, gives a view of the outside world and allows a through draught. *Jali* needs careful handling to avoid breaking the delicate elements of the carved screen. A pattern is marked out on the surface of a slab, pecked out with a punch, then chiselled through. As work progresses the tracery is laid on a bed of sand or stone dust for support. The Red Forts of Delhi and Agra, and even some of the imperial

Left:
Some rock forms may be readily cleaved into flat pieces which are turned into roof slates. Here, heavy, unshaped fragments require the support of a powerful timber structure. Tribal temple in Bastar district, Madhya Pradesh.

Below left:
More sophisticated slate-work. Here, the stone cleaves into thinner slates, each shaped to a rectangle. The ridge always poses a problem. Here, it is rendered watertight by sheet metal, a relatively recent innovation. Kandra district, Himachal Pradesh.

Ridge tiles, Eastern Gujarat. In many parts of India, where transport is simple, light, factory-made tiles are used for the bulk of the roof. The ridge tiles, however, are often locally made: large half-cylinders are shaped and sun-dried over a mould.

buildings in distant Lahore, are faced with this red sandstone. So are the sixteenth-century city of Fatehpur Sikri and many *havelis* in Agra (Uttar Pradesh), Bikaner and Jodhpur (Rajasthan). The fame of Jaisalmer (Rajasthan) rests largely on a plethora of intricately carved houses, temples and palaces of a soft golden sandstone. Easy to work, this is used even for modest housing giving the city its golden hue. Other stones soft enough to dominate local architecture include the yellow limestone of coastal Saurashtra, Kutch (both Gujarat) and the island of Diu.

Mined at Makrana, Kankroli and Udaipur (Rajasthan), white marble graces some of the finest eleventh- to thirteenth-century temple architecture, most impressively in the Jain temples of Mount Abu and Ranakpur (Rajasthan). The Mughals began to use it during the sixteenth century, first in combination with red sandstone, then on its own, most notably in the Taj Mahal. Along with other stones it was often fixed with iron clamps and dowels until, when the metal rusted, it burst apart. Essentially a monumental material, marble *jali* was also in demand for windows and screens in fine *havelis* and to partition formal gardens and terraces. In a vernacular context its importance is as a source of pure lime and *jhinki* (marble powder) used in stucco. Over the past two decades mechanization, particularly the introduction of frame-saws to cut blocks into slices, has made it accessible for flooring and cladding in concrete urban buildings. South Indian granite is too hard to feature in traditional architecture except as rubble or for door surrounds, pillars and steps. Popular for monumental work, it was painstakingly shaped into regular blocks to produce the fourteenth-century Hindu capital of Vijaynagar (Karnataka). A line of holes is drilled by hammering and twisting a long bladed steel rod. A wedge is hammered into each hole until the stone splits. In Hampi (Vijaynagar) the tell-tale holes are ubiquitous.

Along the coast of peninsular India, heavy seasonal rainfall results in leaching, causing iron-rich laterite to build up below the soil surface. A reddish deposit hardening with exposure to air, when freshly dug it is easily shaped into rectangular blocks some 14 by 8 by 4 inches. Laterite is a primary building material in western coastal states such as Kerala, Karnataka and Goa, and is used in all types of structures.

Another hardpan, pale grey in colour, is commonly dug in the North Indian plains. Called *dhandhala bhatta* in Rajasthan, this variety rich in lime was known to the British as *kunkur*. Irregularly shaped pieces, cemented with lime mortar, are used in wall and vaulted-ceiling construction. At its best, it is even shaped into a passable ashlar. More than half calcium carbonate, it is also burnt in open kilns to yield a good coarse lime. Where it is used as a primary building material its availability could even dictate the site of a town. When a group of Shekhawati merchants founded the town of Ramgarh Shekhawati (Rajasthan) in 1791 the choice of site was clinched by rich deposits of *kunkur* nearby.

The Harappans used gypsum plaster with their brickwork and lime was familiar in India well before the beginning of the Christian era. Prior to widespread Muslim influence (from the thirteenth century onwards), however, lime plaster was not in general use. The Muslims introduced it both for mortar and stucco and it was soon an established vernacular material. The country is rich in sources of lime, including shells, which are burned in coastal and riverine areas if limestone is lacking.

In the seventeenth century, stuccowork, associated particularly with Jaipur in the north and Madras in the south, became a fine art. Introduced in palaces and temples, it was soon widespread in smarter houses. This highly burnished white plaster is called *arayish* in Jaipur, or *chunam* (from the Tamil) to the British. Jaipur is looked on as the capital of the craft but, highly labour-intensive, today its use is usually confined to restoration. The technique required a number of coats of hand-ground shell or marble powder mixed with pure lime. This would be applied over a fine plaster, called *loi*, made of ground brick or burnt clay mixed with lime. It was burnished by continual rubbing first with a small trowel, then with a smooth piece of agate. The surface was given a final polish with coconut oil. A variant of this finish formed the *intonaco* (final plaster) on which fresco and secco murals were painted.

Timber was used for most of the early monumental construction in India. As a result little remains of contemporary architecture apart from imitation in rock-cut cave temples or illustration in carved stone and paint. It was not until Muslim rulers imported it that stone and lime-plastered brick became common in domestic architecture.

Over-exploited despite conservationist legislation, timber has become increasingly expensive, thus less used. It survived into the twentieth century as primary construction material for *pukka* buildings in Gujarat and in the south and remains so in Kashmir, the Himalayan foothills and the northeast. Wherever available, it features as the roof supports and joinery in *pukka* and *kachha* housing.

Wooden struts intended to support a projecting roof or upper storey are often made into decorative features. Here, the strut becomes a pari *(fairy) drummer. Mumbai, Jain Temple.*

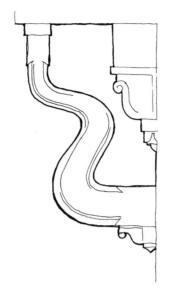

Above:
A carved stone bracket, with half its length set firmly in the fabric of the wall, supports a projecting flat roof. Amber, Rajasthan.

Middle:
Some struts seem impractical as load-bearers and more often serve a decorative purpose. This serpentine form of stone support, inspired by the Hindu toran *arch, was popular in palatial building until the early seventeenth century.*

Right:
Pierced stone screens, jali, *are ancient Indian window forms, allowing muted light and a cooling draught to pass into the building. Islamic geometric forms lend themselves particularly well to* jali.

Joinery is generally simple, confined to variants on the mortice-and-tenon joint. Nails are replaced by wooden pegs, used to join rafters to the ridge or to each other and to hold together wooden stairs. An extended tenon projecting from a tread through the sideboard is secured by a peg. In many parts of the country carved struts supporting balconies and projecting storeys show the most adventurous use of timber members.

Amongst Indian softwoods *deodar* (Indian cedar), the forest tree of the Himalayan foothills, is of prime importance. In Kashmir and Himachal Pradesh many traditional buildings were constructed in alternate courses of stone or brick and massive *deodar* trunks. The flexible timber bonding helped the structure resist earthquakes. Heavily exploited to supply a burgeoning urban demand, the more accessible hills have been denuded of their forests, causing drastic levels of soil erosion.

Much of India's finest nineteenth-century timber architecture was built of *saag* (teak, *Tectona grandis*) in combination with stone or brick. Traditional Gujarati *havelis* evolved using local timber, including *dhak*, but teak, the preferred species, was of poor quality over much of the state. To produce massive timber framing builders turned to the jungles of the Western Ghats, where the monsoon assured high rainfall. Dangs, in the extreme southeast of Gujarat, was once an important timber region for the Portuguese coastal enclave of Daman and is also said to have produced many ships for Nelson's fleet. The hardwood forests of the *ghats* (scarp hills) overlooking the Malabar coast (Karnataka and Kerala), along with those of Burma, were looked upon as the main source of teak for nineteenth- and early twentieth-century Gujarati mansions as well as the palaces, temples and houses of southern India. Strong, resistant to moisture and white ants, teak yields powerful beams whilst the fine grain is ideal for delicate carved decoration. Teak was

seasoned by 'girdling' a living tree, cutting away a ring of bark near the base of the trunk and leaving it to die standing. Demands for shipping and housing proved so great that slow-growing forests rapidly shrank until in the 1860s a programme of planting was launched. The closest rival to teak is the less widespread *anjili* (*Artocarpus hirsuta*).

In North India the role of teak is replaced by another fine timber tree, *saal* (*Shorea robusta*), which grows along the Terai, the plateau rising to the Himalayan foothills. This was exploited not only for houses, bridges and boat-building but also, as the railways extended, for sleepers.

Shisham (*Dalbergia latifolia*), a form of rosewood, is the most widespread timber tree in India and the best for joinery, providing beams and other structural elements. As with all species it is threatened by over-exploitation. In the South, apart from teak, the timber of the jackfruit tree is often used for joinery, whilst *shemmaram* (*Soifruida fibrifuga*) is by tradition popular with Hindus for their houses.

Palm wood, especially from coconut (*Cocos nucifera*) and palmyra trees, is popular for building where available. The timber is strong, flexible but very fibrous – good for ridge beams which tend to curve downwards, battens, rafters and posts; useless for carving. The coconut palm fruits generously for about forty years, after which the tree is felled, seasoned for a year in water, planked and used for timber. The value of its fruit ensures that another tree is planted in its place.

Many other more localized species are also used. In arid parts of Rajasthan, for example, where timber is at a premium, an unpromising little tree producing bright red and orange flowers around the spring festival of Holi was used for carved beams and better-quality woodwork during a *haveli* building boom in the nineteenth and early twentieth centuries. Improved transport allowed it to be replaced by *saag* and *saal*.

The 700 species of bamboo provide some of the richest resources found in the plant world. Apart from the food, fodder and thatch value of the shoots and leaves, the hollow stem lends itself well to a multitude of architectural functions. Belonging to the grass family , bamboos vary greatly in size. Characteristically, the hollow stem is segmented at intervals by nodes, each with a septum (partition) sealing the central space. The starch within the pith is vulnerable to fungal attack and to insects such as the shot-borer beetle.

Bamboo wood, rich in silica, is flexible but extremely resilient. The very form of the stem allows it to serve all manner of functions. The tube can easily become a pipe, a trough, the runner along which a shutter can slide, or the socket for a hinged door. Reduced to splits, it is woven into wall panels. In many places bamboo is woven by a specialized community who sell it in panels. Crushed further, it provides powerful rope, often combined with rattan, to lash the structure together.

India, with some 200 species, is well endowed with bamboo, especially along the Western Ghats and in the hills of the northeast. Where common, it is used virtually to the exclusion of other materials; elsewhere it usually plays some part in the repertoire. Nagaland and Arunachal Pradesh are particularly noted for bamboo architecture.

In those parts of India where bamboo is common, a specialized caste (Kotwadia) weaves panels to a standard height and length, or to order. These are purchased by the householder to provide or renew walls. Bhubaneswar, Orissa.

Even modern non-vernacular constructions turn to traditional wood and bamboo to provide scaffolding; building remains labour-intensive. The individual poles are firmly lashed together. Scaffolding such as this can be seen twenty storeys up on Bombay tower blocks.

Examples of bamboo joinery from northeast India. Sockets are cut in one culm to house another; the joint may be reinforced by cane or bamboo twine.

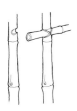

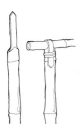
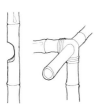

Left:
Domed roof of a Rajasthani jhonpri *before thatching. The structure is created by a radial arrangement of branches set into the wall. Pairs of circular supports are tied together through the domed fabric. Churu, Rajasthan.*

Below:
A bamboo and paddy thatched house built by a caste of professional bamboo weavers awaits plastering. The raised plinth is designed to protect against flooding. Windows are to be provided by leaving sections of the panelwork unplastered. Eastern Gujarat.

Thatch, derived from a multitude of plants, is the commonest roofing material for *kachha* housing. In rice-growing areas paddy straw is preferred. A large variety of monsoon grasses are harvested specifically for thatching. The dried grass is taken up in bunches, and put on the roof in courses, working from the eaves upwards. The ends of the bunches are gently beaten with a flat piece of wood to produce an even fringe. The thatch is then usually tied to the roof frame, either trapped beneath splits of bamboo lashed across the slope or, as in many parts of Rajasthan and Tamil Nadu, tethered by lengths of twine crossing the roof diagonally, consolidating the whole roof. In desert Rajasthan *khinp*, a broom-like plant, is the cheapest source, but soon decays, needing to be replaced annually. Split *kuncha* (elephant grass) is dearer but far more resilient. On the coast dried coconut palm leaves serve the purpose well. The leaflets are also woven together into dense panels, the woody midrib giving rigidity, and used for roofs, walls and fences.

A vital new roofing medium, too well integrated to be ignored, was added to the traditional repertoire during the nineteenth century. Corrugated iron sheeting has been manufactured in India for more than a century. Light, resistant and easy to use, it has superseded many natural materials. Two obvious shortcomings in such a material is that, being metal, it provides very poor insulation and, in areas of high rainfall, resounds with the tattoo of falling rain. In Kashmir and the Himalayan foothills it is ubiquitous, replacing traditional heavy slates or mud-and-dung roofing. It is making inroads on thatch in the northeast. In Bengal it is even occasionally used for traditional curved *bangla* roofs. It imparts status, after initial investment, needs little maintenance and requires only a light roof structure to support it. Another product of the industrial revolution is a metal tile fashioned by flattening an oil can. This is common in hill areas, including Cherrapunji (Meghalaya), one of the wettest places in the world.

Glazed windows are not part of the Indian tradition. In the warmer regions glass inhibits the flow of air in summer. Openings are sealed against winter cold by opaque shutters or cloth screens. Rural housing often lacks window openings, making for an obscure interior. Portuguese colonists were responsible for introducing translucent windows, setting panels of shell some 3 inches square in a wooden framework. Such windows are seen not only in the ex-Portuguese colonies (Goa, Daman and Diu) but also in Kerala. Glass was introduced into traditional *pukka* buildings as a coloured, decorative item. In the 1920s it revolutionized urban architecture as many windows, previously wood-shuttered, started to be glazed, often with frosted glass. Privacy was preserved whilst a new era of lightness dawned upon the house.

UP TO THE ETERNAL SNOW

*Jammu and Kashmir,
Himachal Pradesh,
northern Uttar
Pradesh*

NORTH OF THE GANGETIC PLAIN and Punjab the land rises into the Himalayan foothills, towards the snows. Politically, the hills are divided between the states of Jammu and Kashmir, Himachal Pradesh and northern Uttar Pradesh. Altitude brings a colder climate, but the lower levels are still liberally watered by the southwest monsoon. In response to the cold and a different range of building materials the local architecture differs markedly from that of the plains below. Here, the repertoire is dominated by timber, mostly from extensive *deodar* (Indian cedar) forests, fragmented stone and mud.

The combining of Jammu and Kashmir into one state originates from a British business deal. In 1846, after defeating the Sikhs, the British sold Muslim Kashmir to the Hindu Dogra (hill Rajput) Raja of Jammu, sowing the seeds of a dispute which has soured Indo-Pakistani relations since Independence. The state divides into three ethnically and geographically distinct units: Jammu, the Hindu-dominated foothills overlooking Punjab; the Kashmir Valley, essentially Muslim, a high plateau hemmed in by mountains; and Ladakh, high and dry, populated by racially Tibetan followers of lamaistic Buddhism.

Jammu is a region of subsistence farming, its hillsides terraced to increase cultivatable land. Here, as in most of the hills, unemployment is high and men are drawn to the cities of the plains for work. In the capital, Jammu City, traditional buildings are rapidly giving way to concrete and steel, but in the countryside old ways survive. Substantial buildings are made of the most readily available stone – rounded river or moraine boulders. Partially shaped, these are laid in courses, consolidated with mud or, for the rich, with lime mortar. *Kachha* houses are built of mud brick or wattle and daub, requiring eaves to protect the fabric from heavy seasonal rainfall. This rain supports the dense *deodar* forests which provide timber.

Many of the houses are flat-roofed with an upper storey. The centre of the facade is open, *tibari*-like, with the roof supported on two free-standing and two engaged wooden pillars. The roof of the lower floor, reached by an external ladder, forms its terrace. Heavy beams, sustained by the walls and solid timber columns, support closely spaced joists, the gaps spanned by specially made bricks or, in mud *kachha* houses, brushwood. Over these is laid a bed of mud and gravel between six and nine inches thick which, when dry, is plastered with cow dung. The margin is surrounded by a low parapet of boulders embedded in mud. The roof surface, divided up into rectangular sections by low mud ridges, is used for domestic tasks and drying crops, particularly golden maize. At the margin of this roof a parapet is built up with more river boulders embedded in mud.

Pitched roofs were traditionally tiled with local slates. Some of these cleave into small tiles, but most give thick, heavy slabs requiring a sturdy roof structure. Today slate roofs are rare, replaced by galvanized iron sheeting, despite its obvious practical disadvantages. Equally unsuitable, flattened oil cans are a popular roofing material, commonly used as tiles in the hilly, wetter parts of the country. Thatch is still commonplace, laid in prominent ridges with a slat of bamboo lashed to hold each ridge in place. Brick was used for ambitious buildings: the small one, here known as *Nanak shahi*, has been replaced by the standard brick. This is sometimes used decoratively to form relief arches above window and door openings or even, stepped out course by course, a projecting *chhajja* (sunshade) on the facade.

Decoration also features in the woodwork. There are carved door surrounds, pierced *jali* screens, elegant cusped windows with hinged or sliding shutters, and pillars with attractively shaped capitals. Local mosques sometimes turn to Kashmir for inspiration whilst temples tend to follow a tall-towered, stuccoed Punjabi model.

To the north, beyond the Banihal Pass, lies the Kashmir Valley, over 5000 feet (1500 metres) above sea-level. The Vale and its fringes are rich in timber, which was and remains the primary building material. Tall houses lining the Jhelum River in Srinagar are wood-framed, as are the more handsome mosques, which take a form unique to Kashmir.

Whilst the commonest South Asian mosque plan is rectangular, with a long, blind wall, the *qibla*, facing Meccawards, here the plan is square. Above a foundation of stone set in lime or mud mortar the walls are made of massive baulks of *deodar* set horizontally, alternating with brickwork or stone rubble set in mud. The timbers of one wall are sometimes arranged to alternate with those of its neighbours so that the corners consist entirely of beam ends. In larger vernacular mosques balconies become a decorative feature.

Right:
The Shah Hamadan Mosque, beside the river Jhelum in Srinagar, illustrates a vernacular form quite unlike that of any other region. Square in plan, its foundation is of stone ashlar on which the structure of deodar (Indian cedar) is built.

Left:
The high ceiling of a mosque is supported by pillars shaped from whole deodar (Indian cedar) trunks, each set on a stone base. Jama Masjid, Srinagar.

Left:
A royal barge passes crowds on the banks of the Jhelum river in Srinagar, late nineteenth century. This photograph shows merchant houses as they looked before they were re-roofed in metal. The traditional roof of mud and buroza grass was a far better insulator, but required a stronger wooden frame and frequent renewal.

Below:
The roof of Shah Hamadan Mosque in the background shows the shaggy appearance of vegetation growing on the mud and buroza grass roof.

A few Srinagar buildings still use the old roofing methods. The little stone mosque of Madin Sahib is an example, retaining a rich rooftop vegetation.

The mosque roof is four-sloped with a square turret rising at its centre surmounted by a steep spire and projecting dormer windows. The roof and tower are supported by massive pillars, each fashioned from a whole *deodar* trunk set in a stone base. A *mehrab* (niche) is set in the *qibla* wall indicating the direction of Mecca. Srinagar's Jama Masjid, the city's premier mosque, is a variant upon this theme. Here the square form encloses a large quadrangle, partly a formal garden, centred on a small fountain where the faithful can wash prior to entering the building for prayer. Central to each wing forming this courtyard is the taller spired form of a traditional Kashmiri mosque. The pillars sustaining the domed ceiling of each spired section are some fifty feet high. The result is a large covered area for the city congregation which packs the building on holy days.

Mosque and town house alike used to be roofed by a framework of rafters and purlins on which a skin of birch bark was laid to support a thick layer of mud mixed with cow-dung and *buroza* grass. Once dried this was waterproof and provided very good insulation in a climate of extreme temperatures. Householders even used to grow flowers in their roofing. Until the 1930s the Jama Masjid, the principal mosque, had such a roof until there, as elsewhere, galvanized iron sheets replaced it. Oddly, the traveller William Moorcroft, who visited Srinagar around 1820, describes the houses as being roofed with stone slates. Mud roofs survive occasionally outside the city, easily spotted by the crop of grass covering them. One little Srinagar mosque, that of Madin Sahib, still has its roof of mud and dung, complete with its grass. It also incorporates fine coloured tilework.

The large riverside merchant mansions of
Srinagar are now generally divided among
a number of tenants. They have not escaped
Western influence. The corrugated iron sheets,
gothic and rounded window openings are
derived from British models. But the basic
house, built and rebuilt in brick on an old
timber frame set on an old stone plinth,
follows Kashmiri form. A Hindu temple
sikhara (tower) is covered, in Kashmiri
fashion, with metal plate. In the foreground
are doonga, domestic houseboats.

Srinagar was founded in the sixth century on the right bank of the Jhelum, but crossed the river long since. The founders, Hindu Rajputs, gave way to Muslim Tartars. In 1586 the emperor Akbar took Kashmir, starting a Mughal love affair with the valley. In the first half of the seventeenth century the emperors Jahangir and Shah Jahan came here to escape the heat of the Plains, laying out numerous gardens (most famously the Shalimar) around the Dal and Nagin lakes. But the traditional architecture was affected only in detail by their passing.

Merchants and wealthy landowners who settled in the city chose riverside sites for their mansions because the Jhelum provided a means of communication and freight transport. Recently these houses have been neglected, let out or subdivided, as the rich move to the suburbs. Home to a number of families, the spaces no longer serve their original functions.

In this colder climate a town house is often square in plan, the most efficient configuration to prevent heat loss, without a courtyard. A stairwell ascends the centre of the building. The foundations and plinth are made of stone rubble set in lime mortar, proving so stable that several generations of house may have risen on the same base. The walls of the ground floor, too, are built of jagged stone rubble, not the rounded boulders of Jammu and the foothills, with few and small windows. These have wooden *jalis* (lattices, here formed of closely spaced slats), providing ventilation whilst protecting privacy. More elaborate *jali*-work, known as *pinjara kari*, was used for the shutters of large upper windows until glass usurped its role. This latticework was introduced into the Valley by the ruler Mirza Haidar Shah (1540–51) along with the *hammam* (steam bath).

The main entrance of a town house used to be through a large, wide doorway. It was reduced to its present narrow proportions, so it is said, during the Afghan occupation of the second half of the eighteenth century to prevent horsemen riding in to search for loot. The lower walls were plastered with a mixture of mud, dung and chopped straw, little of which now remains.

Built tall, often three or four storeys high, the upper floors of these town houses are timber-framed with brick filling in the wall. Until Independence the builders used the small lozenge type of brick usual in pre-British India, here known as Maharaji bricks. 'Maharaji' refers to Ranjit Singh, Sikh ruler of the Punjab 1799–1839, whilst 'Nanak', used in Jammu, comes from the founding guru of the Sikh faith. They point to the widespread use of brick being an early nineteenth-century Sikh introduction. The British standard brick was gradually adopted in the twentieth century, incorporated into otherwise traditional buildings. The timber framing includes horizontal, vertical and diagonal elements, forming a load-bearing structure independent of the masonry. In some more dilapidated houses, bricks have fallen from the walls, leaving only the wooden frame. Kashmir is earthquake-prone and wooden-framing is far more resistant to tremors than solid masonry. The brickwork is sometimes laid in a decorative manner, set diagonally, perhaps, to create a pattern.

The main feature of a traditional facade is the *zoondab* (bay window and enclosed balcony). This was either merely cantilevered out from the facade on sturdy beams or also supported by struts. Windows were plentiful in the upper storeys and

Corner of a vernacular Kashmiri mosque, showing a building technique common to this region and parts of Himachal Pradesh: deodar beams alternating with stone rubble above a stone ashlar plinth. The flexible timber bonding helps the building to resist earthquakes.

Right:
A boatman poles a shikara *on Dal Lake, Srinagar. In the background are rows of wooden houseboats, whose superstructures are often intricately carved. Built to accommodate tourists, a family will often live on a* doonga *(covered boat) alongside the houseboat they service.*

Below:
A fluted, lotus-decorated teak baluster from a Kashmiri house. The Hindu lotus form was one of many integrated into Indian Muslim architectural vocabulary.

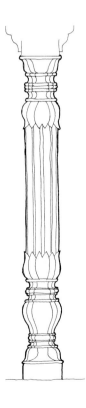

the number of *tak* (bays), each with a single window, into which the facade was divided, defined the house type: it would be identified as 'three-bay' or 'five-bay'. Affluent citizens decorated the interior with carved walnut, cut with geometric or plant motifs, often as separate panels, to be set into the walls and ceiling.

The roof is pitched and, before the advent of corrugated iron, would be made of the same mud mixture overlying birch bark as used for the vernacular mosques. Beneath this now corrugated iron roof is a large hall or *kani*, its ceiling creating an attic of the ridge space. Traditionally, the upper floors are occupied during the summer instead of the lower. The ground floor is a semi-private area where visitors are entertained. It is also used for storage and, along the main streets, houses shops. François Bernier, who visited the valley in the 1660s, speaks of the houses then being all of wood and having gardens. The demand for space in a prospering town soon put paid to most of the gardens.

The same commercial pressure for riverside sites probably played a part in the birth of the houseboat. Boatmen who carried so much of the merchandise along the Jhelum in their *doongas* (covered boats) started to live in them. Perhaps they had always done so; certainly they still do, although their function as carriers of freight has diminished. In 1850 Honoria Lawrence, the first European woman to visit Kashmir, mentions them in her diary:

A great part of the population live entirely upon the water. Long, large, unwieldy boats – thatched over.... An earthen fireplace for cooking, a very rude spinning wheel, a hutch of fowls, a fishing net and a few earthen cooking pots seem the sole furniture.

On the banks of the Jhelum river boatbuilders can still be seen making the traditional *doonga*, its wooden shingle roofing probably a British innovation. The British, like the Mughals before them, fell in love with the valley but local laws prevent non-Kashmiris from owning houses or land. Seeing the houseboats, they were inspired to build their own in order to circumvent the law, to be moored along the banks of Dal Lake or one of the other expanses of water. These houseboats combined the features of a little British bungalow with vernacular construction and decorated woodwork. They line the lake shores, presenting a bizarre selection of pre- and post-Independence names. The owner, living in his *doonga* alongside, lets his houseboat to summer visitors, his family serving the guests.

Most travellers comment on the vernacular bridges of Kashmir, especially those of the city. Seven bridges were built, known today by numbers as well as local names. Their piles were constructed on a cantilever method. Course upon course of *deodar* baulks were set one upon another, each at right angles to that below. Between the timbers river boulders were laid. As the pile rose above water level the baulks running parallel to the roadway were increased in length at each course, gradually narrowing the gap between piles. The space was eventually spanned by more *deodar* beams and a road laid down. So strong were these bridges that one had shops built across it. In 1893 extraordinary floods swept all but one away. British engineers rebuilt them, diverging from the vernacular form by supporting the spans with struts. Elsewhere, suspension bridges were constructed from wood and rope made from sedge, willow or birch twigs, intended only for pedestrians and mules.

The rural houses of the Kashmir Hills have pitched roofs, and, unlike those of Srinagar, are made of large slates, requiring heavy beams. A shallow pitch allows the surface to be used for drying crops. This roof may be built over a flat mud platform forming an attic, often open at either end. It is used for storage of fuel and fodder. The walls were constructed of the nearest usable material, often river boulders mud-mortared within a timber frame.

East of the Vale of Kashmir, isolated by high and hostile passes rising to over 13,000 feet (4000 metres), lies Ladakh, geographically the largest district in India, with its capital at Leh. Known as Little Tibet on account of an ethnically Tibetan population, who are followers of lamaistic Mahayana Buddhism, its culture was protected from advancing Islam by a hostile landscape. A mixture of high mountains and impoverished cold valleys, Ladakh has India's lowest population density. The people grow barley and vegetables and raise yak. Shortage of water confines them to the valley of the Indus and its tributaries. After invasion by the Tibetans in the seventh century Ladakh became an independent state until, in 1842, it was taken by Kashmir. Today, improved access, a large military presence due to the proximity of China and a tourist boom have exposed the Ladakhis to new ideas. They are being drawn into the all-India cultural fold.

The two abandoned royal palaces of Leh and Shey still stand, each said to date from the seventeenth century. Dominating their surroundings and clinging onto bare

Left:
Thin-walled and sometimes boasting alien dormer windows, doonga provide dwellings for a large number of Srinagar folk, reducing the pressure on land along the river bank.

Right:
A row of chorten may often be built near a monastery as memorials to holy men. The form is traditional and the colours often bear symbolic meaning.

Below:
Settlement in a valley north of Leh, Ladakh. The vivid green demonstrates the use of irrigation in this extremely dry environment.

hills, they follow the thick-walled, flat-roofed style common to Tibetan housing on a scale elsewhere only seen in monasteries. The large population of monks and their palatial monasteries here, as in Tibet, has proved a great drain on an impoverished populace. The walls of these palaces were built by the *pisé* method, clay laced with gravel being compacted between wooden shuttering, raised for each course as the previous one dries. Now sun-dried brick is more often used for the upper-storey walls whilst the ground floor is built of roughly shaped river boulders set in mud mortar. The main source of timber is poplar which grows near rivers and streams, and stocks are carefully replanted as trees are felled. Willow, too, is an important resource, used not only for fuel but also in the construction of the roof. Willow twigs are set across the joists before mud is laid.

The family and neighbours are mobilized for house building, making mud bricks on site. Specialized craftsmen are called in for more intricate woodwork and masonry. Construction and the house itself are subject to a number of religious formalities. An *on po* (local astrologer) must ordain an auspicious day for starting work. Then village deities, as well as those of earth, water and other building materials to be used, have to be propitiated. At the entrance three small piles of stones are set up, one black, one yellow or red and one white. Each colour relates to the ethos presiding over a level of the building. Black governs the ground floor, yellow or red the main living level and white the roof and upper floor, seat of the prayer-room and the part of the house in closest contact with the gods.

A Ladakhi house faces south or east, basking in the heat of the sun coming through spectacularly clear air. If built on a hillside, it invariably faces downhill, set in the ground which becomes the back and side walls of the ground floor. The walls taper as they rise, achieved by decreasing the width of bricks used for the upper

Two examples of Ladakhi wooden pillar capitals painted with bright Tibetan/Chinese motifs which support the ceiling in the sitting room of a traditional house.

Left:
Monks' quarters, Hemis Gompa, Ladakh.

Above right:
A flat-roofed building on top of a Thikse monastery, Ladakh, overlooking a courtyard. Auspicious prayer flags and yak tails hang from two poles. Both lintels and balconies are supported by the projecting ends of rafters, breaking the severity of the horizontal lines.

Below right
A typical Ladakhi window opening. A double lintel is supported by rafter ends and the window is glazed save for the lowest panel (glass is a very recent innovation). The window comes down to floor level and people seated on the rugs can conveniently look out.

levels. This gives greater stability but reduces insulation of the upper floors. If brick is used, prefabricated window and doors frames are inserted as building proceeds. With the *pisé* method the walls are built up solid, with lintels integrated into the structure. Openings for doors and windows are cut out after the mud has dried. The ground floor, reserved for livestock in the winter, is ventilated by very small openings. Animals are fed on dry fodder stored on the roof, and help to warm the house through the bitter winter months. They build up a useful store of manure, augmented by a dry latrine from the floor above. This is a small room with a foot-square hole in its floor, with a shovel and a pile of earth to scatter down the hole after use.

The living quarters are on the first floor, reached by a flight of external steps running up across the facade. The entrance leads into a porch giving onto a small courtyard from which the rest of the house is approached, the rooms all opening directly or indirectly onto it. Access to the roof was originally provided by a poplar trunk with notched footholds but this has been superseded by a ladder. The flat roof's parapet is cantilevered out some six or eight inches on all sides, resting on a lintel sustained by the projecting ends of the roof beams. In such an arid climate the roof becomes a usable extra space. It is here that willow wood for fuel is stored alongside the fodder vital to feed livestock through a long, harsh winter. Here, too, is the *chot khang* (prayer room) with the best carved and painted decoration. A carved shrine – usually a family heirloom – holds the chosen deity. With large windows the prayer-room was the best-lit space in the house, before the arrival of glass. Now, some of the better-off have another room, *shel khang* (glass room), on a southern corner of the roof.

The *thabsang*, on the first floor, dominates everyday life. Here the family congregate, cook, eat and sleep. The largest space in the building, it is usually situated in the southeast or southwest corner. The traditional hearth, a simple earthen construction which was the focus of the room, has generally been replaced by an imported iron stove. Above it an aperture serves as chimney and skylight for the kitchen section. Meat is not cooked here but at a separate hearth in the little court. A central column supports the main beam on a bracket which bears dots of barley paste, an offering for the kitchen god.

Furniture is minimal. There may be low tables but chairs are absent. It is customary to sit on woollen mats or blankets. The window openings are very low, providing a view for people who habitually sit on the floor. The right to a *rabsal* (balcony) was reserved for the aristocracy in a rigidly divided society. Before glass arrived the winter cold demanded wooden shutters, condemning the interior to seasonal darkness. But when the sunlight floods in it illuminates a colourful interior. The main decorative medium is paint; interior beams, lintels, window-surrounds and chests for storing clothes are covered with bright Tibetan motifs, closer in inspiration to China than India.

The otherwise austere, almost rectilinear exterior of Ladakhi houses and, on a grander scale, monasteries, is enhanced by accentuating each opening. A lintel is made up of several elements, each projecting one above the other. This serves to heighten the window feature, overcoming the rather unbalanced effect of sills near

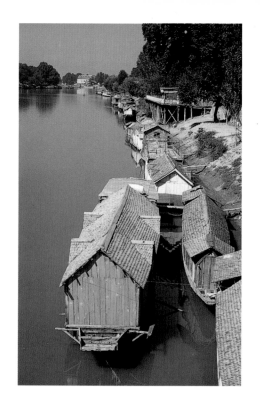

floor-level. The door opening is higher, its lintel interrupting the horizontal line of window lintels and even that of the floor level above.

Monasteries and palaces developed these basic architectural forms using the same vernacular materials. Juniper wood was used for the best interior work. The buildings extend over a hillside from an initial site on its peak. The main structures are imposing, rising to six or seven storeys, a height further exaggerated by the manner in which the complex, as it expands, descends the hillside. Viewed from the front, this gives the impression of one enormous building. The interior is divided to perform various functions. There are cells, halls, chapels, kitchens and open-fronted chambers sheltering *chortens* or large prayer-wheels, or merely used for storage.

Chortens and *manis* are common manmade features in the Ladakhi landscape. A *chorten* is a memorial for a holy man. Square in plan, it consists of a high plinth often stepped in at the top on which stands a solid dome-like structure topped by a tall finial (see picture on p. 51). It varies in size, sometimes spanning a street as an arch or standing with a *mani* beside a track. A *mani* is an unconsolidated wall of stones, each inscribed in Tibetan script with the *mantra* 'om mani padma hum'. It is erected over time by travellers and local folk usually parallel with a road. Tradition demands that it should be passed on the left.

Left:
Thikse Gompa, Ladakh. Monasteries follow the local architectural idiom. Many units are joined laterally and descend from a hilltop site. Windows face southwards; the rear of the building looks to the hillside for insulation.

Below:
Hemis Gompa, Ladakh. The extensively glazed window area is the shel khang, *which has only recently become the showroom of a home, gathering all the warmth and light of the sun.*

Between Ladakh and the plains of Punjab is Himachal Pradesh, a group of Rajput-ruled principalities which became a separate state in 1966. The local culture was subject to a wide range of influences. To the north was a Tibetan Buddhist people, to the west, Kashmir. The princely families of Himachal Pradesh would often intermarry with their caste-cousins of Rajasthan, providing a conduit from that direction. During the first half of the nineteenth century the Sikh kingdom of Punjab held sway here, introducing their interpretation of post-Mughal architectural styles. The British recognized in these green hills a climate, flora and fauna reminiscent of their homeland. They scattered mock-Tudor villas over the countryside in a number of hill-stations, refuges from the summer heat of the Plains, each grouped around its Gothic-style church. In 1864 one of these settlements, Simla, became the summer capital to which the British Viceroy and his government escaped. The local vernacular tradition was exposed to Tibetan, Kashmiri, Rajput, Sikh and British influences, despite which it has managed to retain an individual character.

Prosperous farm houses in the Kulu region reflect some of those in Kashmir, being either all timber or timber-bonded, their thick walls consisting of alternate courses of stone rubble and baulks of *deodar*. They are roofed either with unshaped slates of quartzite or roughly shaped wooden planks.

As elsewhere in the hills, lighter corrugated iron is displacing stone and timber for roofing. In the long term this is impractical because its poor insulating qualities call for increased fuel for winter heating. There is usually a wooden verandah on curved wooden brackets sheltered immediately beneath the eaves. This has a balustrade of little lathe-turned elements supporting a row of cusped arches, a Mughal imprint. Its eaves are fringed with carved wooden pendants. The outer walls are often mud-plastered and the doorway into the ground floor, a cattle shed, is surrounded by an auspicious pattern of red and yellow dots. These houses are two or more storeys high, with a notched log acting as connecting stairs. Enclosed staircases were unknown here prior to British rule. Another Kashmiri feature is the local *sangha* bridge constructed using a similar cantilever method as for those of Srinagar.

There are four vernacular models of temple in Kulu. A carved stone type, generally ancient, with curvilinear *sikhara* (spire), resembles a basic northern Indian model. Two other forms, both still built today, are timber-bonded with pitched roofs of slates or planks. The gabled roof rises to a massive ridge pole (often a whole tree) which is carved into an animal head at either end. One of these, the commonest, resembles no more than a chalet, raised on a stone plinth. The other has a rectangular tower with a gabled roof. The fourth model is pagoda-like, with a series of between two and five superimposed pent roofs above the *garbha griha*. The best example is Hidimba Mandir above Manali. These were probably inspired by similar Nepali temples. The woodwork of these temples is richly carved with angular figurative folk pictures, as on a temple in Gushaini village, some thirty miles southeast of Kulu. Near major temples there is a *bhandar*, the temple treasury in which ritual clothing and masks are stored.

Beyond the Rohtang Pass, in the rain shadow, architecture responds to a drier climate. Northwards, across Lahaul Spiti, a route leads to Ladakh, and Tibetan

Wooden temples in Chamba district, Himachal Pradesh, look to relief carving for decoration.

Above left: The face of Surya, the sun deity, on the high gable end of a temple.

Above middle: A deity, perhaps Krishna, suppressing the evil serpent Kaliya. Votive coins are sometimes nailed into the wood.

Above right: On the roof of an older temple at Chamba, a dancing Persian-style angel looks back to an early form popular for decorating triangular spaces.

Below:
A sangha bridge, supported by cantilevers set in a massive stone foundation on either side of the river. Such bridges were common in Kashmir and remain so in outlying parts of Himachal Pradesh.

architectural forms accompany lamastic Buddhism. Westwards, the Chenab, one of Punjab's five rivers, carves itself a fearsome gorge beside which are villages of flat-roofed mud and stone cottages. Some boast a version of the chalet-type wooden temple, its outer wooden frame enclosing a square masonry shrine. The space between the two structures forms a circumambulatory passage. Its high, steeply pitched roof produces a large unbroken timber gable above an open front. Supported by carved timber lintels and columns, this gable is heavily carved with striking stylized relief figures and patterns.

Lahaul Spiti, the northernmost and largest district in the state, has a mixed population of Hindus and Buddhists. Here, in an arid and often bitterly cold climate, houses are thick-walled, flat-roofed and generally three storeys high. Built close together, in many settlements there are connecting passages between neighbours.

In Spiti houses are generally built in attached pairs. The *kang chimpa* (main house) is for the head of the family whilst his father lives in a smaller *kang chungda*. An unusual local tradition promotes the eldest son to family headship on his marriage. His father retires to farm his own small plot of land.

Kinnaur, the extreme east of Himachal Pradesh, is sharply divided between a lower valley section, which is damp and well forested, and an upper, arid and bare one. The house form is similar in both, but the material used varies. In Lower Kinnaur, with timber freely available, a wooden frame is built, then filled in with stone. Originally no mortar was used to consolidate the walls. In Upper Kinnaur houses were built entirely of mud-mortared stone. An earthquake in 1976 highlighted the ability of timber-framing to resist tremors. The mortality rate in all-stone houses was far higher. Since then, timber has been brought up to Upper Kinnaur to be integrated in the fabric of new buildings.

Kinnaur houses are flat-roofed, usually two-storeyed and face the sun. As so often in hill areas, the lower floor is set aside for livestock which, in winter, help to provide warmth. Local craftsmen, including ironsmiths, also have their workshop here. The upper floor is the living area, surrounded by extended wooden balconies.

Left:
Vernacular wooden temple, northern Himachal Pradesh. Hindus are sensitive to the environment of their shrines. Situated above a spectacular gorge, bright flags enhance the temple's godliness.

Right:
The temple site has been levelled and the priest's dwelling built of dry-stone walling in the absence of lime for plaster.The flat earthen roof, reached by steps, is used as a drying platform. The temple roof is covered with metal sheeting, a recent import. Older temples are roofed with slate and have a considerably flatter pitch. The Chenab river, one of the five rivers of the Punjab, flows through the gorge.

Below:
A modern wooden temple near Kilar, Chamba district, Himachal Pradesh. The facade gable is heavily carved with geometric and stylized figurative motifs. The central core of the building is of masonry, square in plan. The usual single bell, sounded to alert the deity, is replaced here by many bells.

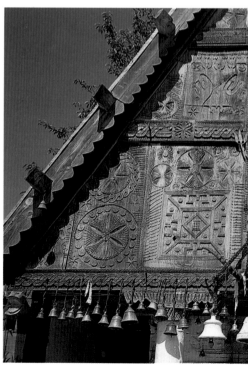

The technology for roofing resembles that of Kashmir: rough planks are covered with a skin of bark on which a thick layer of mud is spread.

In Kinnaur the main beam has ritual significance and, for good fortune, must be set parallel to the main door frame. Prior to the arrival of glass, houses were windowless and dark, with no ventilation apart from a small hole to allow smoke to escape. Each floor consists of a single large space, allowing for no division between sleeping, washing and cooking areas. In Lower Kinnaur the floor itself is made of wooden planks, but in Upper Kinaur mud and dung are used. The *mieling* (hearth) is set in the centre, above it a *dusrang* (hole in the roof) to allow smoke to escape and some light to penetrate. There is always a stone or plank on the roof ready to block the *dusrang* in case of rain or snow. The inner walls are mud-plastered and whitewashed. An *urch* (granary) is built a little way from the main house.

Most Indian societies have some sort of foundation-laying ritual. Here, *prasad* (usually some form of blessed sweet) and alcoholic drink are offered near the foundation stone and at the proposed entrance. After construction is complete there is a housewarming party at which the mason is treated with great respect – lest he curse the building.

The foothills from Himachal Pradesh to the border of Nepal fall in Uttar Pradesh. Seeing their interests and lifestyle at odds with those of plains people, the hill folk agitate for a separate hill state of Uttar Kashi. Rural domestic housing is generally not unlike that of Himachal Pradesh with small cottages of stone fragments in mud mortar, the roof sloping front and back. In villages accessible by road heavy slates have given way to corrugated iron and the better-off build flat-roofed cement houses. Glass has begun to replace the traditional solid-wood window shutters. The main feature of the living space is a hearth. Handsome mud grain-stores, sometimes whitewashed, are also an essential feature.

Most houses are double-storeyed, the ground floor serving as a winter stable for livestock. Often a larger house has a third storey over its rear portion, in which case the first floor roof is flat, providing a terrace for use as a working and drying area in front of the pitched roof of the second floor rooms. Access to the upper floor is by an external flight of stone steps up the side wall. Where a settlement is sufficiently large or suitably sited there is a bazaar, its shops terraced, precluding the usual side steps. Instead, a flight of wooden stairs runs up from the verandah.

During the summer months in the mountains between Kashmir and Uttar Pradesh, Gujar shepherds live at high altitudes. Leaving their families in the winter home, the men take their flocks up to rich alpine pastures. They build permanent single-storey houses as summer dwellings, digging out deep foundations in the side of a slope. The resulting building, half-buried, gives greater protection against the cold. There is only a single space, with the main living and cooking area in the centre of it. The thick mud-mortared rubble walls are unbroken by any opening apart from a low door. As a result, the whole interior is pervaded by woodsmoke. The rear section is used to house cattle when necessary.

The urban architecture of the Uttar Pradesh hills is also influenced by how accessible they are. Some towns close to the Plains – such as Naini Tal, Ranikhet and Mussoorie – flourish as hill-stations and live on summer tourism. They owe their size to the British with their villas, churches, clubs and cinemas. The cluttered bazaar area – the Indian quarter under the old regime – retains traditional features such as wooden facades with cusped-arch openings. The occupants are often Plains folk come to service the tourist industry, however, and they have brought with them both architectural features and an alien use of space.

Temples in Himachal Pradesh and Uttar Pradesh include a number of ancient stone *sikharas* not markedly different from those of the northern plains. What often sets them apart is the lack of any *mandapa* (nave), rather like a spire without a church. Presumably in response to heavier precipitation, this *sikhara* has an octagonal pitched roof perched, hat-like, near its peak. This can be in two tiers, one above and one below the *amla*, a circular segmented section of the upper spire.

Traditional building in the hills, so dependent on timber, has been hard hit by forest clearance. The government, at last taking note of the catastrophic reduction in India's timber resources, has introduced draconian legislation limiting the felling and sale of trees. Although this can be circumvented by bribery it still results in soaring timber prices. Builders are encouraged to turn to substitutes which can be brought up relatively easily from the Plains. So concrete, corrugated iron, standard brick and the urban architecture they favour replace wood and traditional forms.

CHAPTER THREE

NORTHERN PLAINS

*Punjab, Haryana,
Uttar Pradesh, Bihar*

THE NORTHERN PLAINS comprise the Ganges Basin states of Uttar Pradesh and Bihar with Punjab and Haryana to their west. A vast area of rich alluvial land, this represents the most fertile, and hence most populous, part of India. Punjab, the richest state in the country, soared to affluence on nineteenth century irrigation projects: Bihar, the poorest, is subject to the vagaries of the monsoon.

The climate is continental, ranging from little more than freezing of a January or February dawn to well over 40 centigrade (104 Fahrenheit) in May and June. This relentless summer heat is broken by the southwest monsoon which, from early July, waters the fields for some two months. Sometimes it fails; sometimes it is overgenerous. The rural population relies on a moderate monsoon for the autumn crop (*kharif*). Winter rains supply another in spring (*rabi*).

The Harappan civilization, the earliest in the subcontinent, reached Punjab and western Uttar Pradesh, bringing the first urban grid planning and the courtyard house. On the banks of the Ganges the Aryans, long after they swept the Harappans away in around 1500 BC, set up towns. In Bihar during the sixth century BC two great teachers, Mahavir, founder of Jainism, and the Buddha, rebelled against religious order. Here rose the Mauryan Empire (321–185 BC), based at Patilaputra (modern Patna), to spread Buddhism. Its fall was followed by a sequence of invasions, setting a pattern which lasted into the eighteenth century. The Northern Plains were a honeypot, drawing marauders from the northwest. Many stayed to rule.

During the early days of man's presence, the Ganges Basin was richly forested, so timber played an important role in large-scale building, dictating its trabeate form of vertical posts and horizontal beams. A growing populace in search of agricultural land cleared the trees to till the soil. Alluvial clays were used to make sun-dried and kiln-baked brick, which has dominated the architecture of the region ever since.

The cities are islands in a vast, productive flatness, subject to seasonal inundation and drought, barely broken by low earth ridges, the field boundaries. Across green crops or sharp dry stubble, clumps of trees denote settlements. A young village lies flush with the surrounding landscape. Ageing, it rises, climbing out of the plain on the detritus of its forebears. Centuries pass and it crowns a substantial eminence, sufficient to protect it from flooding. Each year, swollen by the monsoon and melting snow, the great rivers stretch over the land, enriching it, bringing fertility and death.

A Plains village follows an ancient Vedic plan probably drawn from nomadic encampments. High castes build by right in the centre, forming a nucleus. The social scale descends towards the village fringe. The lowest in the hierarchy – leatherworkers, sweepers, scavengers and tribals – live 'beyond the Pale', outside the village boundary.

Above left:
In the Terai area, Kangra, Himachal Pradesh, where the plains rise to foothills, rainfall is heavy, and rock outcrops provide an important building material. The stone is shaped for slates and paving, or used unworked for dry-stone boundary walling.

Above:
Timber provides pillars, panelling, window shutters and a low balustrade on the sheltered upper verandah. The balcony has to be partly supported by two secondary pillars. Kangra, Himachal Pradesh.

Below left:
To save internal space a flight of steps has been built on the outside of the house, giving access to a storage area beneath the pitched roof. The slates have been extended to shelter the steps.

A house-form the Bengalis call aat chala (eight-slope) which gave rise to the British colonial bungalow form. The central core is often a single high room whilst the low outer area houses sleeping space and a kitchen. The building is constructed on an artificial terrace. Nadi, Himachal Pradesh.

Rural housing of the Ganges Basin has changed little over millennia. Two-thousand-year-old carved reliefs show circular and rectangular thatched huts much like those of today. Near rivers, the flood-plain villager adapts to circumstance. Aware of the futility of confronting the goddess of the river he builds a light, thatched shelter of brushwood, bamboo and straw, lashed with twine and plastered with mud. The flood destroys it effortlessly. The fragments are salvaged, the structure resurrected. Truly vernacular, these buildings utilize nothing from beyond the immediate vicinity.

On higher ground it is possible to build with greater permanence. Here, the walls are of sun- or kiln-baked bricks, or are built up in courses of mud and dung. In the east the roof is pitched, tiled or thatched with paddy straw. In Punjab and Haryana it is generally flat, surrounded by a low parapet. Each household aspires to an open semi-private area. The poor make do with an adjoining patch of ground, which is swept, or slightly raised. Recognizing this as their compound, visitors remove their footwear at its margin. Some wall off an area with bamboo wattle or a hedge of brushwood. A wealthier farmer encloses the area with mud walls, sometimes topped with thatch or tile to protect it from rain, or with inward-facing buildings. One of these serves as a porch or gate. This provides a place where visitors can socialize.

A compound or courtyard setting for domestic life is an important feature of most Indian housing. Here grain is husked, ground to flour, dough kneaded, *roti* (unleavened bread) and vegetables cooked, vessels and clothes washed. A little mud *chulha* (stove), constructed by the women, constitutes a kitchen, out of bounds to those of lower caste.

If there is space livestock are brought in at night to the shelter of a byre. The family bathes here in a sheltered corner, clad in sari or undershorts. In the courtyard a *mandap* (small awning) is set up, under which marriage takes place. A corner is dedicated to a deity often housed in a mud shrine facing eastwards.

Almost all the daily ritual takes place outside or, during the rains, in the shelter of a verandah. The *jhonpri* (hut) provides shelter from the elements, for night privacy and storage. It is an ill-lit refuge, an area of darkness. There are no windows, but sometimes ventilators. In warm weather people sleep in the compound, often on a mat of bamboo splits, covered either with a cotton *chaddar* (sheet) or, in winter, a *razai* (quilt). These are stored in a corner of the hut. A *charpoy* (bedstead, literally 'four-feet') is the most common item of furniture. It has a wooden frame over which a lattice of twine or cotton tape is tied. The parts are all jointed and are easily taken apart. The *charpoy* functions both as bed and bench. Here, the ancient patriarch sits in the sun, smoking his *hookah* whilst one of his little grandchildren massages his aching legs.

Within the house, the most striking items are the *kothi* (grain stores). Built of mud and dung, either in courses or on a basketwork frame, a *kothi* stands on four stubby legs, out of reach of rats. The bottom is reinforced with wood and a plugged hole allows the contents to pour out. When full, the top is sealed. The largest, often set outside at the edge of the compound or, in prosperous houses, in a separate granary, holds the local primary grain – wheat in Punjab, rice in Bihar. Smaller *kothi* hold other grains and pulses. Like most mudwork, they are fashioned by women of

Left:
The cooking area of a Bihari kitchen. Two mud chulhas (cooking fireplaces), side by side, are formed so that round-bottomed vessels can perch securely over the flame, whilst the fire is well ventilated. Mud cupboards and jars are used for food storage. Madhubani, Bihar.

Below:
Grain stores are often beautifully moulded in clay over a basic wood or basketwork frame. The large one on the right holds the staple grain, probably rice. The structure on the left juxtaposes small grain stores (the sealed compartments) with shelf space. Grain is poured into the sealed area through an opening in the floor of the shelf, to be taken out through a sealed opening in the lower front (best seen on the top right, where it has been resealed with cloth). Madhubani, Bihar.

the family and are often decorated. In Madhubani (Bihar), famous for craftwork, small *kothi* are sometimes shaped humorously as fish or animals.

The only fixed storage space is a low loft under part of a pitched roof, formed by bamboo or wooden poles bridging the room. These are usually not fixed. Here, farming implements are kept. More valuable possessions, such as the best clothing, would always be put in covered baskets. These have been replaced by a small metal trunk which frequently features in dowries. Wealth in the form of jewelry is worn by the womenfolk as heavy bracelets, anklets, necklets and earrings, always ready to be pawned to the moneylender. Any other jewelry, along with money savings, is generally buried under the mud floor. Other possessions, including everyday clothing, are hung on pegs or from the rafters. If the wall is brick or course-laid mud, inset niches are used for small items and little glassless oil lamps. This constitutes the only source of domestic light in much of Bihar; in rich Punjab few places lack electric light.

Almost a fixture by virtue of its weight, a *chukki* (handmill) is set on the verandah or in a corner of the compound. It consists of a thick disc of stone set in a depression cut into another of greater diameter. The upper disc has an upright handle near its edge and a hole in its centre through which grain is poured.

Few villages boast tapped water, although the government's recent large-scale programme installing handpumps has brought a safe source nearer home. Otherwise, water is carried by women from a well, out of bounds to lower castes. In rural Bihar, where caste conflict is particularly bitter, low-caste folk risk death by taking water from a high-caste well. Lacking one of their own, they must make do with the local pond or river. The morning queue at pump or well is one of the main social events in a woman's life. Water, in terracotta pots, is stored in a shady part of the compound. In northern Bihar this may be an oval recess shaped into the high mud plinth of the house.

A private corner of the compound is set aside for urination, otherwise the lavatory is wasteland around the village, well served by pigs. They fatten themselves on faeces before being devoured in turn by the lower castes. Women 'go outside' before dawn, each bearing her *lota* (little water vessel, often brass) or bottle of water. Men go later. On return each fastidiously washes hands and *lota*. When urgency demands a foray in broad daylight both sexes' modesty is protected by selective blindness: they are just not seen.

Apart from wells, the only communal structures are places of worship. If the caste or religious constitution of the village varies then neither can be assumed to be common to all. Focus of all religious festivals and perhaps an annual fair, a place of worship reflects the wealth of the community. A mosque can be simply a wall oriented to face Mecca with a *mehrab*, a niche for the prayer-leader, at its centre; a temple can consist of a shrine flying a red pennant, containing some small image.

There is a rich tradition of decoration. In Punjab some mud walls are covered with relief work known as *sanji*, incorporating pieces of glass and coloured foil. The Santhal tribals of southeast Bihar divide their walls into blocks of red and yellow ochre. In Madhubani district (Bihar) Brahmin and Kaisth caste women are celebrated for their stylized figurative work. In preparation for marriages and

Left:
Plains village house, raised on a plinth against flooding. The verandah provides a sheltered workspace, with a handmill for grinding flour. A cooking chulha stands in the courtyard. A pot in the mud wall holds drinking water. Bunches of paddy straw for thatch dry on the roof. Madhubani district, Bihar.

Above:
Doorway to a courtyard, revealing Roman-tile roof. Hand brooms stand by the door. Above, water pots serve as a dovecot. Arki, Bihar.

Below:
Rice paste decorates the entrance. Projecting rafters provide useful pegs. Arki, Bihar.

festivals they adorn verandah walls and those of the honeymoon room with pictures illustrating Hindu myths, especially those relating to Rama and Krishna. During the Bihar famine of the mid-1960s they were taught to paint for the commercial market, using bright poster colours on paper. The resulting work took Delhi by storm.

Relief designs are common. Some are textural arcs simply made by a sweep of the plasterer's hand; others are complex patterns of finger- and handprints combined with pinched outlines. These can be functional: handprints or sets of concentric circles embellishing an outer wall deflect the 'evil eye'. In some regions when a child is sick it is customary to make an effigy using an amount of cow dung equal to the child's weight. This is applied to the house wall. As it dries the sickness is supposed to retreat and should be cured by the time the dung falls to the ground.

Across the plains cattle dung is the most common fuel. Avidly collected by women, it is shaped into discs and clapped onto a convenient surface to dry. The discs are then neatly stacked into a form varying with local custom – conical or cylindrical in Punjab and Haryana, rectangular, hut-like, in western Uttar Pradesh. As the stack rises it is closely walled with mud and dung, a roof finally closed over it, sometimes even thatched. Known as *bitoda*, these structures look like tiny dwellings, standing either in a group within the village or near the owner's house. In western Uttar Pradesh and parts of neighbouring Rajasthan their walls are wildly decorated with relief plants, flowers, peacocks – anything appealing to the woman's eye.

Buddhist relief carvings and rock-cut caves in Bihar, Madhya Pradesh, Maharashtra and Andhra Pradesh provide a glimpse of early Indian urban architecture. Characteristic during the Mauryan period was a *chaitya* arch, rounded and culminating on its outer surface in a raised ridge. Constructed of shaped wood, it was supported by a framework of shaped and horizontal timbers, faithfully recorded, though functionless, in cave monasteries. Two other Mauryan forms developed: a *stupa*, or brick hemisphere built over some relic of the Buddha, and magnificent Ashoka pillars, monolithic shafts of fine stone from Chunar (Uttar Pradesh) capped with the figure of some beast.

The Gupta Empire (320–550 AD), centred on the Ganges, gave birth to a typical northern Indian temple form: a hall with a sanctum, topped by a *sikhara* (spire), at its west end. Variants on this, with a rectangular or cruciform *mandapa* (hall) in front of the *garba griha* (sanctum) to shelter devotees, is dominant throughout all but South India. Even when creating soaring temple *sikharas*, Hindu architecture clung to trabeate methods of construction with horizontal posed on vertical, each held in place by its own weight and that of elements above. Early in the second millennium their inherently heavy appearance was visually lightened by a mass of lively figurative sculpture. During the twelfth century repeated Muslim invasions checked the northern Indian temple's evolution.

Islam taught an antithesis of Hindu architectural language. Structural form was primary, celebrated at the expense of decoration. Figurative carving was taboo. Dramatic pointed arches, arched vaults and domes, each using the shape of individual stones to spread the load, became widely used across the land.

The Mughal heartland was here, in the Plains, with capital cities at Delhi, Agra, Fatehpur Sikri and Lahore (now in Pakistan). The impact on traditional

Right:
A wattle-and-daub wall in the process of being mud-plastered. Here, the women have decorated their work with a relief design. Madhubani, Bihar.

Below:
On a mud wall which shows the textural arcs of the sweeps of the woman plasterer's hand, stylized beasts are painted in bright finger impressions. Rajwar, Sarguta, Madhya Pradesh

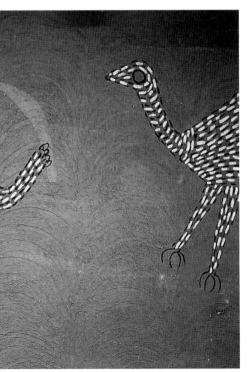

architecture of seventeenth-century Mughal technology and form was powerful and has persisted.

The *Shastras* (religious treatises), although laying down regulations, say little about the appearance of domestic buildings. It is not until the sixteenth and seventeenth centuries that accounts by foreign travellers mention details of towns and their constituent parts. The Frenchman François Bernier, writing of Delhi in the 1660s, mentions the

> habitations of the Munsebdars [officers] or petty Omrahs [nobles], officers of justice, rich merchants and others; many of which have a tolerable appearance. Very few are built entirely of brick or stone, and several are made only of clay and straw, yet they are airy and pleasant, most of them having courts and gardens, being commodious inside and containing good furniture. The thatched roof is supported by a layer of long, handsome, and strong canes and the clay walls are covered with a fine white lime.

There was a good reason for a successful official to build cheaply, in mud: on his death his property reverted to the throne. There was a good reason, too, to spend more on furnishing: that might escape the imperial hand and reach his heirs. Under British rule *seths* (wealthy merchants) displaced Mughal nobility in northern and central India as the main patrons of *haveli* building. The *haveli* form reached its zenith under the new regime.

An era of prolonged peace brought prosperity. Towns and cities burst their walls. Most surviving fine townhouses were the products of the nineteenth- and early twentieth-century mercantile wealth often accrued from colonial trade. The power and excesses of Hindu and Muslim rulers had been curbed, although they continued to control forty per cent of the country. The foundations were laid for a thriving middle class. A commoner who prospered need no longer look over his shoulder in fear of an unbridled tyrant. The climate of stability and security encouraged fearless architectural display. The nineteenth century became the great era of *haveli* building. There were few constraints apart from capital and availability of material.

A fine family home, once completed, no longer reverted to the government on the death of its owner: it could pass down through generations. The builder's name would be glorified by his descendants for the great house he had bequeathed. A *haveli* must be large since his honour depended in part on the number of relatives he housed and supported. He also had to plan for an ever-expanding joint family. All his sons would bring their wives back home, and their sons, in turn, would hope to do the same. Some *havelis* originally consisted of a single storey, but the walls were made massive enough to bear one or more additional levels to accommodate the growing family.

These merchant *havelis* were constructed in the *bania mohalla* (merchant caste sector) of a busy town, their courtyards pools of peace, sheltered from the frenzy of urban life outside. Despite their size and opulence they were traditional structures, planned and put up by a team of local builders drawing on materials available from the surrounding countryside. In the great northern alluvial plain this implied burnt

Left:
One of India's most ancient living temples,
built on the site of Buddha's enlightenment.
The layout grew out of rural vernacular
design: a house centred in a fenced compound.
The structural elements take on monumental
form, with a towering sikhara and a boundary
fence of red sandstone. Boddh Gaya, Bihar.

Above:
The interior of rural housing is dark and
ill-ventilated. All is sacrificed in favour of
temperature regulation. The upper wall is
often left unplastered to provide rudimentary
ventilation; the lower section is plastered and
often decorated either with colour or textural
designs. Bamboo is used for the frame of a
paddy-thatched roof. Plains villages are often
dotted with fruit trees – a papaya stands on
the right. Madhubani, Bihar.

Right:
Fish are a common motif on either side of
the upper door in both monumental and
vernacular buildings. In Oudh (Uttar Pradesh)
they were once the totem of the ruling
dynasty. Above the door, Ganesh, Lord
of Beginnings, casts an auspicious light
over all who enter a Hindu homestead.
The guard and elephant are usual doorside
figures through much of India. Varanasi,
Uttar Pradesh.

brick, timber and lime plaster. Today a client expects accurate architectural plans, but then a practised builder would only sketch out an approximate layout of rooms, following customary form.

Tradition, rather than conscious effort, allowed this plan to conform with religious injunctions laid down in the *Shastras*. Only when considering the facade were any detailed drawings made. Innovation was incorporated merely in superficial features – the shapes of openings, shutters or decorative stuccowork.

An archetypal northern Indian town house is *chaukband* (built around at least one courtyard). The concept of a courtyard, an enclosed private space open to the sky, is basic to Indian urban housing. A building turns inwards onto this secret interior into which few are privileged to pass. There is a second, semi-private space where guests can be freely taken. In the great *havelis*, this is a forecourt. In a smaller Hindu household the sexes are separated by distance or, in a Muslim one, by warning women to retreat from sight on a stranger's arrival. The visitor is taken into a room and the women resume their tasks. Since Independence, with

increasing emancipation, strict rules of *purdah* (literally 'curtain'), which kept well-to-do married women out of sight of non-family males, have become more relaxed, and the inner courtyard's privacy has been reduced. It remains the heart of a house.

Thanks to natural decay of brick and woodwork, few extant *havelis* predate 1800, so early evolution of the form is obscure. Recent examples owe much to Mughal tradition. A rare Mughal ruin at Sirhind (Punjab) is rectangular in plan, consisting of two blocks of rooms linked by high curtain walls to enclose a courtyard. Externally it presents a forbidding expanse of blank brick wall broken by a pattern of rectangular recessed panels. Only at the southwest end does the full height of the building remain, topped by a curved, vaulted *bangla* (Bengali style) roof. Its projecting *chhajja* (eave) shelters all that remains of a plaster finish once decorated with floral murals.

This western section, open to the exterior, was the *mardana* (men's area). A door leads to a series of domed chambers outside – the *hammam* or baths: 'Turkish' baths were an Islamic introduction adopted in some Hindu *havelis*. The eastern block, set away from the entrance, was a *zenana* (women's area). A view of the private courtyard from the entrance is denied by a right-angle turn in the access.

This layout typifies that of a nineteenth-century mansion. A courtyard forms the focus. External walls, although decorated, give an air of defence and privacy. Mughal decorative roof forms are already integrated into domestic architecture. Typically, a shading *chhajja* (eave) supported on stone brackets runs the length of the facade, sheltering the main and usually only entrance. This is through a large arched gateway closed by two massive, metal-reinforced doors. Hinged on stone sockets, one or both leaves hold a little wicket door, allowing access without opening the main gates. At either side of the gateway is a small platform where *chowkidars* (watchmen) would sit. Always on duty, they would sleep in a chamber in the gateway. Informal household business is often conducted in the shelter of this gateway.

The entrance gives onto a semi-private forecourt, with *dalans* (open-fronted chambers) giving onto it through three cusped, or pointed, arches on one or both sides. This is the *mardana*, open to male business and casual visitors, who are entertained in one of the *dalans*. Traditionally, furniture is absent, the floor being laid with thin mattresses covered by white cotton sheet. Here, men recline against *masnad* (large bolsters) as they converse. Metal rings are fitted in the ceiling. Today redundant, they once carried a *punkah* (fan), a wood-framed strip of cloth moved back and forth by a string held by a servant outside the room. Other rings above each arcade provided attachments for screens. In winter these were of heavy quilted cotton often bearing a red and white chevron pattern; in summer *chiks* of bamboo splits or *khas* roots were kept wet by an attendant. Evaporation cooled the room whilst pervading it with a pleasant scent.

One room, the *diwankhana*, large and well decorated, is intended for formal entertainment at marriages and festivals. This is outside the women's permitted area, but they have access to a special mezzanine floor of tiny low rooms, looking onto the hall below through small screened arches. Invisible, they could see and hear.

Sikh builders took up Mughal architectural forms and led them away from the purity of simple forms to more indulgent decoration. The double-cusped arch, in stucco above and on either side of the door, is flattened, with rows of decorative lotus petals. The jharokha, *or balcony, provides grandeur above the entrance. The general layout is one common in North Indian houses: an open balcony overlooking a door. Punjab.*

Guests arrived on horseback or in a *rath* (covered bullock cart), coming into the forecourt. The inner courtyard is raised, with steps leading up to the door. Although generally it was closed, even if open it gave no view into the *zenana*: a screen wall blocked the back of the porch, penetrated by a tiny window or *jali* (lattice). A visitor jangles the chain used to secure the door and an older woman checks his identity through the spyhole. They converse thus, she barely visible. Few men outside the immediate family could approach further. Today the sexual division has weakened and, in the company of men of the household, it is easy to pass into the inner court of a Hindu *haveli*.

For a large part of her life the courtyard is still a woman's whole world. Here, she performs domestic tasks, eats, sleeps, bathes and, in a room set aside for the purpose, gives birth. The kitchen is dark, ill-ventilated and cramped, marked by soot stains around the door. In contrast is the airy space, called the *parinda*, used for storing terracotta pots of water. This has a window and a *jali*-work door. A through draught keeps the water cool.

Women prepare and cook food crouching at ground level. There is no dining room. The *thali* (little tray) of food is carried to the menfolk wherever they may be. When the men have eaten the women can follow suit. On formal occasions diners sit cross-legged on mats, their *thali* placed on a *chauki* (low wooden platform) before them.

Rooms giving onto the *chauk* (courtyard) function as bedrooms and stores. Those of the lower storey are open *dalans* behind which are closed rooms. Internal masonry stairs lead to the upper storey and the flat roof. The upper rooms are reached by a narrow projecting walkway supported by stone brackets set in the wall.

Few rooms have specific functions. In the absence of furniture today's bathroom can be transformed into tomorrow's kitchen, bedroom or store. The floors, covered with fine waterproof lime plaster, slope towards a drain. Drainage is essential, particularly for Muslim bedrooms: the faith decrees that a couple must bathe after intercourse.

The flat roof is an important space, cool on summer nights, where the family socialize and sleep. Sockets around the roof allow for bright *shamianas* (awnings) to be erected there. Another attempt to escape the heat is a *teh khana*, a cellar beneath ground level. Although poorly lit, it maintains moderate temperatures.

In the plains *havelis* are built of brick consolidated with lime plaster. Above the rooms, beams support closely spaced joists, the gaps bridged by flat bricks on which a thick layer of mortar and rubble is laid. The roof is finished with fine lime and slopes gently around drains to spouts which carry water clear of the walls.

The lower floors are virtually blind to the exterior, the only openings being small ventilators. Upper rooms have shuttered windows. The facade is decorative, its surface divided by relief stuccowork in the form of pilasters and cusped arches. In Uttar Pradesh, influenced by the European architectural forms adopted by the Kings of Oudh in the late eighteenth and early nineteenth centuries, the decoration includes triangular and rounded classical pediments, fluted pilasters with Corinthian capitals and plant forms. In Punjab wooden *jharokhas*, elegant covered balconies with finely carved *jalis* (lattice screens), project from the facade.

Tall merchant town houses in Hardwar give onto a narrow bazaar. The ground floor is occupied by shops. The first floor projects over the street, supported by carved toda *(stone brackets). The facade is enhanced by characteristic relief stuccowork taking architectural forms. At the top of each floor a sheltering* chhajja *(eave) projects. The houses on both sides are probably in the ownership of one extended family, who can cross by the bridge without entering the street. The households are serviced by a multitude of itinerants, such as this tinker.*

Most of the historic towns of northern India still flourish. They are subject to a demand for space which has wrought destruction on now-outmoded mansions. *Havelis* are either divided by unsightly walls to provide cramped housing for many families or have been demolished.

Other towns, losing their importance for one reason or another, have shrunk. Relieved of pressure, old *havelis* can gradually sink back into the earth. Narnaul (Haryana) is one such backwater. A once-flourishing Muslim district capital, it finally declined at Partition. The better-off Muslim population left for Pakistan or fell victim to religious riots. Their houses remain, some with courtyards raised eight to ten feet above porch level, reached by a stairway on one side. This difference of level serves to isolate a semi-private porch from the private inner court.

Farrukhabad (Uttar Pradesh) declined for other reasons. Once a busy river port, it thrived on grain trade until the mid-nineteenth century, when railways arrived. The train passed it by and the river meandered away. Today, fine bathing *ghats* (stepped masonry banks) descend into an emerald expanse of wheatfield. In the town several handsome but dilapidated *havelis* remain.

The port lay in what was then Oudh kingdom where, in the late eighteenth and early nineteenth centuries, the court adopted European classical architectural styles and decoration. Their assimilation into domestic buildings is reflected in Farrukhabad's *havelis*. The layout is traditional but post-Mughal decoration is sprinkled with Palladian forms. A deeply cusped archway with stucco floral work around it makes a feature of the entrance, but the wooden louvred shutters above seem strangely Parisian in style – although such shutters may exist only in stucco or paint as *trompe l'œil*. Some openings are topped by stucco triangular or rounded pediments. Fluted pilasters entwined with spirals of 'ribbon' and Corinthian capitals separate panels of Hindu religious murals. The plasterwork is sometimes painted with an ochre brickwork design. The odd habit of concealing bricks, then painting a brick motif on the plaster, started in early seventeenth-century Punjab. On either side of most gate arches is a relief of a fish. This was the ruling family's symbol but, while those of Uttar Pradesh are the largest, similar fish reliefs are common in northern India.

The traditional *haveli* features remain in place – a wide *chhajja* (eave) supported on stone brackets shading both doorway and courtyard, open three-arched *dalans*, a carved wooden door surround with iron-inlaid shutters and, in Hindu houses, an image of the elephant-headed god Ganesh, Lord of Beginnings, overlooking it. An increasing intrusion of Western motifs into vernacular forms persisted into the twentieth century. Then reinforced concrete swept the traditional urban house aside, replacing it with a ubiquitous and functionally inappropriate glorified box.

Just across the border in Pakistan, Lahore, which was long capital of undivided Punjab, boasts several fine Sikh period (1799–1849) *havelis*. That of Dhyan Singh, erstwhile ruler of Jammu, is built on a monumental scale, its entrance more like that of a fort than a town house, recalling troubled times. The layout of *dalans* turning onto a vast courtyard with underground *teh khana* (cellar) and a *hammam* (Turkish bath) parallels that of Oudh. What sets Punjabi *havelis* apart, whether in India or Pakistan, is decorative woodwork on the facade. Characteristic are *jharokhas*

Left:
Havelis *(mansions) of affluent Oudh
merchants turned to Mughal monumental and
Western classical architecture for decorative
forms. Triangular pediments take their place
uneasily beside cusped arches. An impressive
gateway leads into the semi-public forecourt.
Above the massive reinforced doors a room
is often used for entertaining 'outsiders'.
Stucco deities (Durga on a lion, Saraswati
on peacock, Ganesh in the apex of the arch)
guard the entrance. Painting in ochres
further glorifies the entrance. Farrukhabad,
Uttar Pradesh.*

Above:
*The doorway to a merchant townhouse
is made to resist assault. The thick timber
leaves are heavily reinforced with iron and a
powerful bolt slides across to be locked firmly.
The platforms at either side of the door were
intended for the* chowkidar *(watchman).
Electricity has arrived characteristically in
a web of wires. Old Delhi.*

(enclosed balconies) from which the women of the house could overlook street life. They were often roofed with a segmented dome, a post-Mughal form common in Sikh architecture. Beneath this are little cusped-arch openings protected by carved wooden *jalis* which let in light but prevent intrusion. Punjab is prosperous, its older buildings suffering badly as a result of neglect in favour of new buildings.

Founded as Shahjahanabad by Shah Jahan in the second quarter of the seventeenth century, the old city of Delhi was famous for its fine houses. After the British suppressed the 1857 Mutiny they carried out fundamental alterations to the damaged city. Its *havelis* often belonged to Muslim aristocrats, natural supporters of the last Emperor of the Muslim Mughal dynasty, Bahadur Shah, who was raised as a figurehead by the mutineers. The British felt no qualms about demolishing their old *havelis* to make way for improved roads and railways into the city. Hindu merchants, who prospered under British rule, took over from the aristocracy as *haveli* owners and builders.

The smaller town house follows a *haveli* model and is frequently referred to as such, especially by the owners. Its functions had to be compressed into a single courtyard. The urban poor build on the city's edge; their houses, of the cheapest materials, are set out in village fashion along winding *galis* (alleys).

As the twentieth century progressed labour became more expensive and traditional materials, particularly timber, became dearer. After Independence cement and steel girders, cheaper and bearing the cachet of modernity, took over as the primary building materials for Indian urban housing. The overwhelming fashion was for Western forms and an ever-extending electric grid, bringing with it cooling systems, made this possible. Traditional architecture was ignored as rustic.

Improved public transport and the private car made it possible for the wealthy to escape the congested town centre. But the modern affluent suburbs do not bear a strong Indian cultural imprint. A trend towards nuclear rather than extensive joint families means that smaller houses are in demand. Little remains of the old *chaukband* plan in the concrete architecture of the 1960s and 1970s. Some houses retain a courtyard but most do not. Only recently have the urban rich started to demand houses that reflect local forms and traditions. When they do so it is not merely from nostalgia: practicality is involved.

Inside the old town gates, now absorbed by the city's expansion, caravansarais were built. This is an Islamic institution and recent sarais owe much to Mughal architecture in layout and decoration. Writing in the 1660s the French traveller François Bernier mentions an example in Delhi:

The Karuansara is in the form of a large square with arcades, like our Place Royale, except that the arches are separated from each other by partitions, and have small chambers at their inner extremities. Above the arcade runs a gallery all round the building, into which open the same number of chambers as there are below… Hundreds of human beings are seen in them [sarais], mingled with their horses, mules and camels. In summer these buildings are hot and suffocating, in winter nothing but the breath of so many animals prevents the inmates from dying of cold.

Sarais were built by wealthy philanthropists as safe shelters for camel and bullock caravans, the pre-rail freight carriers, and as cheap shelter for travellers. A large courtyard is enclosed by one or two storeys in which are both *tibaris* (three-arched open chambers) as well as rooms with doors. The gateway must accommodate a laden camel or even elephant. It is sealed by massive double doors, which may be passed through a wicket set in one or both leaves. At the centre of the courtyard a tree provides shade. Here, free or for a nominal fee, travellers spread out their bedding to sleep in comparative security.

Sarais, now usually known as *dharamshalas*, are still constructed, maintained by a trust or a wealthy Hindu merchant. Today, apart from serving as an inn, they house any visiting *baraat* (marriage party accompanying the groom to his bride's town). It is incumbent on the bride's family to accommodate and feed the *baraat*. They book a *dharamshala*, where the bride's male relatives serve their guests.

The nature of Hindu faith precludes memorials: death is only transitory absence from earthly life. Monuments are seen as the products of a man's lifetime – temples, gardens, wells, tanks or sarais. While in most cases (though not all) the corpse is cremated and ashes consigned to some river, preferably the Ganges, memorials were not altogether unknown. Indian Muslims, contrary to the tenets of their faith, were great tomb builders. The Taj Mahal, built by Shah Jahan for his wife the empress Mumtaz Mahal, is the foreigner's commonest perception of Indian architecture.

Little domed tombs, usually square or octagonal, are scattered throughout the country. Wealthy Hindus adapted the custom to their own use, raising a *chhatri* (literally, umbrella or parasol, the traditional shelter for royalty and gods) on the cremation site of a relative. This is a masonry dome containing a dated inscription. Its neck is generally octagonal and rests on eight free-standing pillars. The first *chhatris* appeared around Delhi and Agra in the sixteenth century. The form was soon widespread in northwestern India.

The domestic architecture of the north Indian plain has been little affected by post-Independence industrialization. Vernacular materials such as mud and paddy straw remain the cheapest available and perform their tasks efficiently. Dearer materials – standard burnt brick and corrugated iron sheeting – bring with them prestige rather than utility. The cities of the plain expand, drawing in the rural poor in search of a living. They form slums on the city's edge, reproducing familiar house forms, defiant of planning, with sticks, cans, cloth and polythene sheeting. These have become urban vernacular materials, the detritus of a twentieth-century industrializing nation.

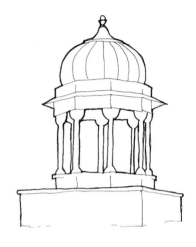

Above left:
A caravansarai was a fixture near the entrance of most large North Indian plains towns. The buildings remain, often still providing cheap shelter for travellers. On either side of the entrance small shops open onto the street. The main gate, which allows people to enter via a wicket, is large enough to admit a laden camel. A tree in the centre of the courtyard provides shade for man and beast. Rooms open onto the courtyard.

Above right:
The chhatri *form developed in the fifteenth century as a Hindu answer to the Muslim tomb. The dome is erected over the cremation site of any Hindu whose relatives are rich enough to pay for it. Generally it stands on eight pillars set on a raised plinth.*

CHAPTER FOUR

THE DESERT WEST

Rajasthan,
northwest Gujarat

THE WESTERN STATE OF RAJASTHAN is cut by the Aravalli Hills which form a spine running from northeast to southwest, dividing it diagonally. To the west is arid sandy desert, poor millet-growing land ploughed by camels; to the east, better-watered, richer soil yields wheat and vegetables – even sugar cane. Banni, a desert tract in the extreme northwest of Gujarat, adjoins it, with its own desert culture.

Rajasthan (literally 'land of rajas') was divided into a number of principalities, mostly ruled by Hindu rulers of the Rajput caste. At Independence the Hindu princes acceded to India. Resigning their sovereignty, the new constitution granted them pensions commensurate with the wealth of their estates. The little kingdoms were united to form Rajasthan.

Until the eleventh century this desert formed an impassable barrier. Then the technology for sinking deep wells was developed and busy caravan routes grew up, punctuated by these new watering places. Camel- and bullock-borne trade linked the Ganges Basin directly with that of the Indus, bringing prosperity to settlements along its path.

The infertile hilly border between Rajasthan and Gujarat, to the south, supports a mixed population, partly made up of Bhil tribal folk, descendants of pre-Aryan inhabitants. Agriculturalists predominate, their extra needs served by potters, carpenters, tailors and shopkeepers. There are also nomads – Banjara, once important transporters of goods; Bawaria, still hunting with bows; and Lohar, tinkers who live in and around their spectacular carts.

Rural desert architecture is remarkable for sculptural shapes, achieved in mud. West of the Aravalli Hills from Shekhawati, through Bikaner and Jaisalmer south to Barmer and Banni in Kutch, this often dramatic mudwork dominates the villages. House form varies, with a trend from a rectangular plan, prevalent in the north, towards a circular one more common in the south. Prosperous folk often mark their enhanced status, hoping to escape their rustic roots by abandoning the traditional in favour of a box of brick, cement and stone planks. These materials are also imported for government village schools or clinics.

Initially a house consists of a single enclosed space, a circular or rectangular hut. More are added as the family grows and prospers. This results in a collection of structures, each independent but related, standing together in a compound or sharing a common platform which raises a semi-private area above its public surroundings. The group of buildings face into an increasingly private space enclosed by a mud wall or brushwood hedge. Thus a courtyard is created.

The complex develops for individual convenience, free of fixed rules. Each building is oriented in relation to its neighbours, not towards any specific direction, although the household shrine is generally in the east.

A jat *(farmer caste) house complex, Churu district, Rajasthan. The two small buildings in the foreground (left and far left) are* kothi *(grain stores); the largest contains millet, the local staple. A child stands on one of two mangers. The circular thatched building in the background (centre) is one of several, each functioning as a room, opening onto the inner courtyard. The woman is about to enter this space. The rectangular building on the right is to house guests; it faces outwards, away from the privacy of the courtyard. (See also the plan on page 82.)*

Typical is a Jat (farming caste) compound house in Binasar village near Churu. Four circular huts about ten feet in diameter form the corners of a private courtyard. Along one side, between two of these, is a small rectangular room with a pitched roof. On the east side stands a little mud shrine. Another rectangular room on the south side, its back forming part of the courtyard wall, projects outwards, opening onto the semi-private fenced area, a substitute forecourt. This is the guest room, excluding visitors from the intimacy of the family. Two mud *obari* (grain stores), one for *bajra* (millet), the other, smaller, for *moth* or *moong* (pulses) stand at the edge of the courtyard. The courtyard contains the main hearth, a mud *chulha* (stove), as well as *chulhas* for heating milk and fodder. Outside the courtyard but against its boundary is an enclosure for livestock at night, fenced with thorn branches.

Many villagers express a preference for a circular building, claiming that it is stronger and more resistant to summer winds. A wall, usually about six feet high, is expected to last some twenty to thirty years. A circular trench is dug and posts set up to support it. The wall is made flat on the ground as a mat some 15 to 20 *hath* (hands) long, using brushwood from a bush called *jhari*. It is held together by double bands (one outside, one inside) made of *roira* twigs or *akra* stems. Two bands are close together at the foot, one at the top of the wall-mat. The two parts of each band are stitched together through the brushwood of the wall with a large wooden *suwa* (needle). The 'thread' is made from *khinp*, a common broomlike plant. A mason is often summoned to make the roof: in any case he supplies the 'needles'. To make a roof the wall structure is merely extended to form a dome.

In Hindu architecture there is a preference for odd numbers of architectural elements, a custom followed even in these huts. The structure of the dome consists of nine or eleven horizontal bands made of bunched grass, supported by twenty-one similar ribs. One of the ribs, stronger than its fellows, is lashed to the structure forming door jambs.

Thatch is of *kuncha* (elephant grass), dearer but long-lasting, or *khinp*, which must be renewed every other year. Thatching takes a single day, as does plastering with mud and dung. A twine of split elephant grass binds the thatch to the horizontal bands within the dome. Another form of needle, hook-shaped and of iron, is used to stitch the thatch to its supports. Unplastered circular huts are seen isolated in fields across northern India. These are stores for fodder and shelter for men watching over the crops.

Around the desert town of Jaisalmer, the three-foot-high walls of rectangular houses are built by women in courses of stone fragments and mud. Mud bricks, measuring around 12 by 8 by 2½ inches are also used. Once the wall has dried a roof frame is added, unshaped branches being used as rafters, their thick ends forming the ridge. Since good timber is scarce, a ridge pole, often curving up to the centre, is fashioned from small branches lashed together. Each rafter is made of two branches, one extending down the inside of the wall, the other outside. These are bound so that together they grip the wall. At ridge level the rafters of both slopes are jointed, the end of one being whittled to form a slot into which the other can fit snugly. A hole is cut through the male element and through it a peg is fixed to hold the joint firm. The rafters are bound to each other with twine made of *khinp* and

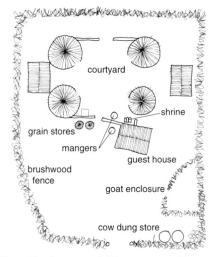

Plan of jat *homestead. The compound is surrounded by a fence. Two rectangular and four round rooms open onto the inner courtyard (below). The photograph on pp. 80–81 was taken in front of the grain stores.*

Right:
Rectangular houses on the fringe of a small town. The roof is made as a mat, then lashed over the rafters with homemade twine. Camel carts (on the left) are a post-Independence innovation, pneumatic tyres being necessary to run over desert sand. Jhunjhunu district, Rajasthan.

Below:
Inner courtyard of jat *homestead (see plan, left). A child sits on a* charpoy *(bedframe). The frame serves as a seat by day.* Khinp *(broom) thatch secured by* khinp *twine only lasts a couple of years before beginning to collapse, as in the hut on the left.*

twigs are fitted into the roof fabric. Finally the roof is thatched with *murat*, a grass which grows during the monsoon and is suitably dry by February to April. This is the main building season, following the cold winter and preceding the busiest agricultural season.

In larger houses the buildings combine with a wall, often topped with geometric mud *jali*-work, to enclose a compound for domestic work. The walls are decorated with ochre patterns, invariably accentuating the doorway.

Banni, a small expanse of flat, arid grassland in Kutch, relates more closely to desert Rajasthan than to the rest of Gujarat. Pastureland dependent on a fickle monsoon, Banni projects into the glaring white salt flats of the Rann of Kutch, once the delta of the mighty Indus. It supports a small population of cattle raisers, spread out in hamlets, who until recently moved freely but illegally to and fro across Pakistan's frontier. They married and smuggled between the new states. Ninety per cent of the people are Muslim Jats (farming caste), the rest low-caste Hindus.

Hamlets consist mostly of circular *bhunga* huts, arranged in clusters according to subcaste allegiance. There is no street plan, only paths that wander through the place, causing the houses to turn away for privacy. Each dwelling comprises several buildings, with round *bhungas* providing the living space, and smaller, rectangular *chokis* as rooms for washing, cooking and storing water. These are linked by a platform, *otla*, raised some 18 inches above the surroundings and used for all domestic chores. It replaces the compound, being open rather than closed.

Houses are built of clay, rough branches and thatch. A *bhunga* is three to six yards in diameter, its wall constructed from sun-dried mud blocks. The conical thatched roof projects on all sides, resting more on a beam supported by two external posts than on the walls. In front of the door a verandah provides a sheltered working area.

Left:
Kutch is justly famed for its mudwork and embroidery. The womenfolk use every utensil as an object of display, a contemporary equivalent of the Mughal chini khana *(china rooms). Banni, Kutch, Gujarat.*

Below:
The interior of a bhunga *(circular hut) shows the women's decorative handiwork. A large clay cupboard, richly set with mirrors, dominates the room. Most of the wall surface is covered with relief abstract and figurative motifs. Banni, Kutch, Gujarat.*

Right:

A bhunga *(circular hut). There are no windows and the entrance is sheltered. The conical roof is constructed of roughly shaped branches supported by several large uprights positioned outside the walls. Thatch is lashed over this frame. Generally there is no walled compound, the semi-private area around the house indicated merely by a raised mud platform. Charpoy bedframes serve as seats and beds. Bharandiria, Kutch, Gujarat.*

Below:

An extension supported by unshaped forked poles covers the entrance as a porch. Painted mudwork accentuates the door, which may be secured with a chain padlocked to a fixed ring on the lintel. Pegs project on either side of the door, whose panels bear auspicious swastikas. In rural India shoes are always removed before entering a house or holy place.

Outer walls may be painted in ochres with flowers and abstract designs. The interior is more impressive, the walls covered with relief decoration set with mirrors. Kept spotless, the clay floor rises into several platforms where it meets the wall. One, opposite the door, is called a *pedlo* and on it stands a grain store quite unlike those elsewhere in the intricacy of its mudwork. Perched on four legs, the whole surface is covered with shaped patterns and little mirrors. Other similar structures, but with wooden doors, are used for storing possessions. In the space under these containers and in recesses in the wall utensils are kept.

Banni women are famous for their needlework, especially hangings for the house and bright appliqué *dhadki* (quilts) for winter bedding. These add a colourful touch to an already beautiful interior.

Parts of Rajasthan are rich in stone. At Makrana and Kankroli white marble is plentiful. Grey marble there and elsewhere is an excellent source of lime. Fine sandstones outcrop near Bikaner, Jodhpur, Jaisalmer and in the extreme east towards Dholpur, where red beds are coupled with smooth buff ones. Some of these stones are strongly bedded, cleaving into long, thin *patta* (planks) which have revolutionized building since improved transport has made them widely available.

The Pukka House

In Rajasthan the best-preserved collection of early urban housing is in Amber where several seventeenth-century *havelis* exist in various states of dilapidation. They survive due to a radical move by Raja Jai Singh II, who, in 1727, deserted the town to found a new capital, Jaipur, six miles away. Amber became a backwater with no demand to replace old houses with new.

The remaining *havelis* are three or four storeys high, around a courtyard with *dalans* (open rooms). Some upper rooms are capped with *bangla* arches, domes or four-slope pent roofs. They are constructed from stone fragments and brick, worked stone being used for pillars, brackets, balconies and pierced *jali* windows. Ceilings were built on scaffolding, a vault or dome of bricks set on edge in concentric circles consolidated with strong lime plaster. Such ceilings were widely used by the Mughals. The custom of building vaults on a wood and brushwood scaffolding, common until the mid-twentieth century, results in little vaulted rooms typical of drier parts of the state. It absolved the need for suitable timber for beams and rafters. Today, stone *patta* and steel girders create large, flat-ceilinged rooms. Anyone who has experienced both types of roofing in all seasons knows that massive vaulted ceilings deal far better with Rajasthan's enormous temperature range, providing sufficient insulation to soften its extremes.

Some Amber *havelis* have decorative mirrorwork, consisting of small fragments assembled to form peacocks, or vases of flowers, set in the plaster walls of the *baithak* (sitting room). Introduced to India by the Mughal Emperor Shah Jahan (ruled 1628–58) and now firmly integrated into western Gujarati mudwork, this was a Syrian fashion. In Amber it is inspired by the beautiful seventeenth-century *sheesh mahal* (glass salon) of the Palace, which overlooks the town. A pattern is set out on paper, and thin pieces of mirror carefully cut to form a jigsaw. The outline of each

Sandstone patta *(planks) from local quarries, trimmed into regular shapes and ready for use. Recent improvements in transport have made these widely available materials, changing the nature of local building. Rajasthan.*

Right:
The structure of a *Kutchi* bhunga, *unlike that of a Rajasthani circular hut, has a structure of unshaped branches supported by a central pole and by others outside the walls. These are lashed in place with twine, the interstices filled with brushwood over which thatch is laid. Ludia, Kutch, Gujarat.*

Below:
Open lattice windows, jali, *are particularly important in the desert region where sunlight is harsh and summer temperatures high. Here, a grid pattern contrasts oddly with the cusped frames, but gives an uninterrupted view of the magnificent scenery beyond. Amber, Rajasthan.*

Decorative techniques in Rajasthan include the use of fresco painting, relief plasterwork and stencil. Colours reflect the surrounding land, in reds, yellows and greens.

Left:
The unplanned city of Amber, once capital of Rajasthan (later moved to the planned capital, Jaipur). The far hill is crowned by a protective fort. Beneath it stands the palace whilst the walled town huddles in the valley, around its fine mosque (centre) and temples. Where possible the townhouses enclose a courtyard, focus of all the rooms, and where most of the household tasks take place. The roof is used for storage, but also as an extension to the rooms. In summer people sleep on the roof to take advantage of the cool breeze, with low walls providing some degree of privacy. Here, beneath the hills, stone rubble forms the primary building material.

piece is perforated through the paper with a needle, making a *khaka* (stencil) to set against the wet plaster surface. This is dabbed with a cloth bag of soot, transferring a dotted outline of each glass fragment which could then be set into its correct place. The same stencil technique is used for wall painting, already a popular form of decoration in seventeenth-century Amber. The palette was usually limited to red, yellow and green earth colours.

Nearby Jaipur is a magnificent example of early eighteenth-century town-planning, overseen by Vidyadhar, a minister at court. In siting the city he deferred not only to Raja Jai Singh but also to the leading Brahmin priests of the kingdom. The town was built on a plain immediately south of a high hill. Laid out on an approximately square grid plan, the city's axis is a wide boulevard running east to west from Suraj Pol (Sun Gate) to Chand Pol (Moon Gate). Craftsmen came to build and service the new city and merchants to set up business. If high walls defended by massive bastions and street plans were directly in the architects' hands, individual houses were, subject to certain restrictions laid down by Vidyadhar, the responsibility of their owners.

There are impressive *havelis* in the city based on two or more courtyards, but many have suffered from modernization and division. Those of Shekhawati, their direct descendants, have mostly escaped this fate. The city temples, raised high above the streets, are reached by a long flight of steps, with a door giving onto a courtyard. There are two types, one typical of North India, standing as a free-standing chapel-like structure with a *sikhara* (tower), surmounting the *garbha griha* (central shrine) and an adjoining *mandapa* (aisle), sometimes cruciform in plan with a domed chamber at its junction. The second is vernacular, dispensing with a *sikhara* and borrowing from contemporary *haveli* design. The courtyard has *tibari* (three-arched chambers) on each side, but there is no building in the central space except possibly for a little Hanuman shrine. On the west or east side a *tibari* forms a vaulted porch, its axis at right angles to that of the temple, often heavily decorated with wall paintings. Beyond is the *garbha griha*, in front of which hangs a bell to announce worshippers, and around it a corridor for circumambulation, an essential part of a visit to the deity. The building is single-storeyed, with the remaining rooms used as the priest's dwelling and for storage. Its facade, like that of an eighteenth-century *haveli*, is decorated by arched pavilions and domes on slender stone pillars along its roof. This temple design became widespread in eighteenth- and nineteenth-century Rajasthan but the present tendency is to return to the spired model.

It was during the reign of Jai Singh that his relatives, rajputs of the Shekhawati clan, having evicted several *nawabs* (Muslim rulers), extended their hold over the region now known as Shekhawati. This comprises the present-day districts of Jhunjhunu and Sikar. The region was especially significant because of the caravan trade routes that crossed it. When the Shekhawati barons reluctantly accepted Jaipur's suzerainty they insisted on retaining several points of independence, including the right to set duties levied on merchandise crossing their borders. By the close of the eighteenth century, war and instability had drained princely treasuries, so the Rajas of Jaipur and Bikaner enormously increased excise rates. Together their states created a wall of high tariffs across all northern Rajasthan – all, that is, save

Shekhawati. Here, the barons kept duties low. Caravans concentrated on this corridor, as did the merchants who profited from them.

In 1819 the two Rajas, under advice from the British, sharply cut their duties. Overnight the diversion through Shekhawati became unnecessary. With trade irretrievably damaged some merchants migrated to benefit from a radically altered pattern of commerce. Through Calcutta, the British capital, flowed raw materials for export from the vast Ganges Basin and imported goods destined for its markets. Young Shekhawati traders moved down the river and, as brokers to British businessmen, grew to control almost all trade through the city. During the nineteenth and early twentieth centuries the merchants repatriated some of their vast fortunes to finance an explosion of conspicuous building in Shekhawati and neighbouring Churu. New towns were founded, some modelled on Jaipur. Since that age of prosperity there has been little pressure for space, so a visible architectural sequence survives.

Previously, local trade brought affluence to a handful of families, supporting a few large mansions. It was no time to draw attention to one's money. Most of the business caste lived in small, terraced courtyard houses. In 1818 the Rajas of Jaipur and Bikaner, along with many of India's princes, recognized British paramountcy, giving them power to curb princely excesses and bringing to an end interstate wars. Rich merchants were encouraged to settle in British-administered territory and given guarantees of protection for holdings in their home state. After decades of insecurity, the Banias (merchants) felt able to display their wealth.

A *seth* (wealthy man) aimed to build five principal structures – a temple, a memorial *chhatri* (a dome supported on pillars) to his father, a *haveli*, a caravansarai and a well. The building boom drew masons and labourers from Jaipur and its surroundings and they used the materials closest at hand. Along the Aravalli Hills in Singhana, Khetri and Jhunjhunu stone fragments set in lime plaster formed the fabric of the walls. In Nawalgarh, Lakshmangarh and Sikar, where suitable clay and fuel was available, brick was preferred. In the heartland of the region, Mandawa, Bissau, Fatehpur and Churu, a light grey hardpan, *dhandhala*, lay just below the surface. Lime-rich, this was used in roughly-shaped lumps as ashlar and burned for coarse lime. Stone elements such as paving, balusters, pilasters, *chhajja* (projecting eaves) and *toda* (supporting brackets) are still mass-produced at several hillside quarries, particularly at Raghunathgarh near Sikar. Fine limestone came from quarries near Nawalgarh and even powdered sea shells, carried 800 miles from the coast, were used for the best stuccowork.

The earliest surviving Shekhawati *havelis*, dating from the close of the eighteenth century, were blind and defensive on three sides. Square *choubara* (roof-top rooms) on each corner could function as turrets from which armed men were able to protect the walls. On the facade a certain amount of ostentation was allowed – perhaps a decorative arch above the gateway. There were small, shuttered windows on the upper floor and some stucco decoration, often painted in ochres. Early *havelis* usually had a wood plank ceiling in the porch, sometimes bearing the date of construction. This disappeared during Shekhawati's building boom between 1860 and 1920 when all ceilings became vaulted. A large *baithak* (sitting room) was

created by using a carved timber beam to support two *dhola* (vaulted ceilings) side by side. Later, iron girders resolved the problem. With increased peace and political security buildings expanded, decoration became more ambitious and defensive features less obvious. The layout was unchanged but the arch over a balcony above the entrance disappeared. Only walls giving onto the street were finished with stucco decoration and paintings. Others remain roughly plastered.

Mural paintings in Shekhawati are a major tourist attraction. They decorate *havelis*, temples and *chhatris*. Any walls facing the road and those of courtyards are likely to be painted but the finest work is in a display room, the *rang ka kamra* or *rang mahal*. This is usually on the first floor above the courtyard door. Most rooms have a painted dado, consisting of framed blocks of colour. The traditional pigments were red, yellow and green earth colours and lamp black. For finer work red lead, natural ultramarine, vermilion, copper chloride, silver and gold were used. The external work was executed by a technique known as 'Jaipur fresco', which results in tenacious pictures. Some even remain bright on outer walls of seventeenth-century buildings. A thick layer of pigment is worked into the damp surface of a final plaster of pure lime. The colour is partially trapped in the surface during the carbonation process. The pictures were burnished with pieces of polished agate and finally wiped over with coconut oil. Another form of decoration was to incise patterns into a painted surface to reveal white plaster, a variation on the scraperboard technique.

Painters are mostly drawn from local *chejaras* (masons), both Muslim and Hindu. Skilled draughtsmen used a stylus to incise outlines of figures and patterns in the damp surface, sometimes with the aid of construction lines. The team then paint, area by area, struggling to keep up with the plaster's drying.

Left:
A bedroom of a haveli *above a courtyard. This section of the room may be curtained off to create a small separate* tibari *(three-arched chamber). All the surfaces are finished in a highly burnished stucco, known locally as shimla. Storage niches and wooden pegs are for clothes. Bissau, Shekhawati, Rajasthan.*

Below:
Shekhawati merchants and Rajasthani rulers built extravagant memorial chhatri. *Here the dome is raised above a basement of rooms including a Shiva temple, set on a high plinth. Decorative pavilions and domes surround the main* chhatri. *Mahansar, Rajasthan.*

Right:
The former fort of a Shekhawati baron now extends to house a growing family. Flat roofs serve as summer bedrooms. In the background is a cremation area with the chhatri *(pictured below). Mahansar, Rajasthan.*

A different method is used for fine interior work. The design and figures are carefully set out, usually freehand, on a dry surface. Repeated figures such as marching soldiers, camels and horses are sometimes stencilled. Paints are applied using plant gum as a binding medium. Mural painting using this technique is widespread in North India. As the building boom passed the demand for such painting faded and today the method is rarely used except for restoration.

Shekhawati *havelis* resemble those of the Ganges Basin, always aspiring to, if not achieving, two courtyards. A visitor would drive his *rath* (covered bullock cart) up a ramp and through a high arched gateway into a semi-private forecourt. Onto this a *baithak* opened through three arches, its floor covered with the customary mattress and white sheet. Here, guests or business contacts would sit, leaning against one of the large, firm *masnad* (bolsters).

The doorway to the inner court is set directly opposite the main gateway or at right angles to it. Relatively small, it is reached by a flight of steps. The arched recess over the door often bears the best wall paintings in the house, showing the coronation of Ram or the marriage of Krishna. The surround is well carved, usually in wood or, in some towns, in stone. Presiding over the entrance of all these Hindu *havelis* is a figure of Ganesh carved into the lintel or set in a recess above it.

The door can be locked by a fixed chain which, when rattled, serves as a bell. It gives onto a porch with, at its back, a screen wall pierced by a small window or *jali*, protecting the courtyard's privacy. Entry beyond this wall was until recently restricted to women visitors, close family members or intimate friends.

The courtyard is paved, except for its centre, which is left as sand to be used as an abrasive for cleaning dirty utensils. A little pillar-like structure holds a sacred *tulsi* (basil) plant. *Tibaris* (chambers opening through three arches) give onto the courtyard on one or more sides. The kitchen (there is often more than one) is in a corner, the wall above it stained with soot. A special room, the *parinda*, is intended for storing terracotta pots of water. Its small *jali* window and door of beautifully carved *jali*-work allow the air to circulate, keeping the water cool.

Above left:
A palatial hall follows the pattern of a baithak *(sitting room) of a* haveli, *with three-arched* tibaris *giving off it and screened windows on the mezzanine floor from which women can spectate. Samode palace, Rajasthan.*

Above right:
Finely decorated chhatri *dome. In the outer* rasamandala, *Krishna miraculously seems to be dancing with each of the many* gopis *(milkmaids). The inner ring juxtaposes scenes from Krishna's life with those from the* Ramayana. Ramgarh, Shekhawati, Rajasthan.*

Right, top: Facade of a traditional haveli, *with shuttered windows and a projecting storey. Three-arched platforms by the door shelter the* chowkidar *(watchman). Massive iron-faced doors allow a bullock cart to pass.*

Middle: The semi-private forecourt. On either side a three-arched baithak *opens. The rooms are vaulted, sometimes with a double-vault supported in the centre by a massive beam.*

Bottom: The private inner courtyard. On the roof, a pedkala *shelters the stairwell. Tibaris open onto the courtyard. A pot contains the sacred basil plant.*

Far right:
The inner courtyard of a haveli, *now home to an extended family. Three-arched* tibari *open on either side. A married woman's life is traditionally confined within this courtyard.*

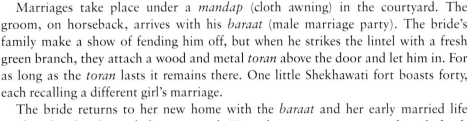

Marriages take place under a *mandap* (cloth awning) in the courtyard. The groom, on horseback, arrives with his *baraat* (male marriage party). The bride's family make a show of fending him off, but when he strikes the lintel with a fresh green branch, they attach a wood and metal *toran* above the door and let him in. For as long as the *toran* lasts it remains there. One little Shekhawati fort boasts forty, each recalling a different girl's marriage.

The bride returns to her new home with the *baraat* and her early married life rarely takes her beyond the courtyard. Here the women prepare and cook food, bathe, wash clothes and utensils. A little door may give onto a *nora*, a narrow compound running along the side of the house. This is used as the women's lavatory, serviced by the sweeper caste. For men the surrounding countryside serves the purpose. Today, concrete purpose-built lavatories often deface buildings.

A *jina* (stairwell) houses the steps which lead up to a walkway connecting upper rooms, then on to the roof where it emerges under a tiny shelter, or *pedkala*. Of a summer evening, men sit on top of this playing *chaupad* (a form of draughts) or chess, enjoying the cool breeze.

Furniture plays a small role and rooms are not rigidly tied to a function. Wooden *charpoys* (bedsteads) are easily moved. Many of the family escape the summer heat by sleeping on the roof, which is surrounded by a high parapet wall. Here they lose privacy but benefit from the cool breeze. Married couples could use a bedroom known as *chandani* (*chand* means moon), half of which is a tiny courtyard, open to the sky. *Chandani* became redundant towards the close of the century, perhaps due to the increased number of windows in the upper rooms.

Thick masonry walls give these desert *havelis* excellent insulation. The mercury ranges from 50 degrees centigrade (122 Fahrenheit) down to below freezing. Iron rings set in the masonry were used to suspend screens and cloth *punkahs* (fans).

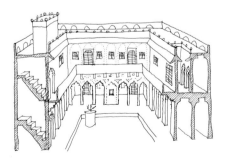

When I first visited Ramgarh in the mid-1970s one cloth fan still functioned in a bazaar teahouse, activated by the toe of the proprietor.

Even in such a small area there is a tendency towards local variation in style. Probably due to pressure of space Churu's *havelis* grew upwards rather than outwards to become the tallest in the region. In Nawalgarh the facades are often oddly aligned with the street, the doorway parallel to it, but the wall set off at a slight angle. In Fatehpur variation comes, as so often, in murals. A large panel of Lakshmi, goddess of fortune, showered by elephants with liberal use of deep blue ultramarine, is the local favourite.

One of the five architectural ambitions of a wealthy man was to build a *chhatri* for his father. Money was of little object to great *seths*. A large plot of land on the edge of town was walled in as cremation site for an individual or a family. Here they built their *chhatris*, raising one or more domes on a considerable basement of rooms. That in the centre often enclosed a Shiva temple complete with *lingam* (phallus). An inscription commemorated the dead man. A Shekhawati *chhatri*, at its best, is more than a passive memorial to a successful man. The land was open to the public, both it and the building serving a living function. A *chowkidar* (watchman) was responsible for the memorial, and travellers and pilgrims could camp in the *chhatri* rooms. A well stood in the compound and often an *akhara* (wrestling ground) developed, where young men could fight and excercize. Distant in concept from an austere graveyard, the *chhatri* became a focus of life and activity – to the greater glory of the dear departed. Great *chhatris* are no longer built, but those standing are often used as primary schools. The domes are filled with childish laughter and chatter – a beautiful cenotaph.

Rajput palaces, including those of Udaipur, Bikaner, Jodhpur and Bundi, have become a complex of variations on an initial symmetrical core. Enclosed within massive fortificiations, they spread across a hilltop or down its side. Earlier palaces retain Hindu forms, trabeate structures, square-based octagonal or square pillars with bracket-like capitals supporting stone lintels. *Chhajjas* project from the side of courtyards and out over facades. Windows, especially in a *zenana* section (for women only), peep from behind stone *jalis*. Decorative elements often relate to the lotus bloom, derived from ancient Buddhist motifs. There are friezes of petals or reliefs of the whole flower, some later integrated into Mughal vocabulary.

But the flow of Mughal architectural idioms was overwhelming. From the early seventeenth century onwards they invaded, sweeping aside heavy trabeate in favour of arcuate forms. Balusters replaced octagonal columns and supported ubiquitous cusped arches, a juxtaposition reflected in stucco relief. The building's outline shows further borrowing in its domes and *bangla* roofs (themselves borrowed, as the name suggests, from Bengal). Rajasthani *havelis* followed this trend. The fashion for red sandstone and white marble made inroads on local materials. Highly burnished white stucco-covered interiors. This stucco is often credited to the Mughals, but they picked it up in Gujarat. Other aspects of the interior were influenced. Although murals decorated palace rooms in earlier times – traces survive at Chittor – a Mughal taste for floral dados and figurative work replaced an older tradition. The synthesis evolved towards a distinctive Rajput style of art. All palaces have a *sheesh*

mahal (glass apartment), its walls set with a mosaic of mirror fragments. Mirrorwork reached India from Damascus, appearing first in Shah Jahan's Sheesh Mahal in Lahore (Pakistan). Hindu rulers imitated, Mirza Jai Singh's effort at Amber Palace being sufficiently good to put the Emperor's nose out of joint.

Rajput architecture followed Mughal into decadence. During the nineteenth century it imitated that of British rulers. The final examples are massive post-Victorian piles quite independent of any defensive wall. Modelled on rural palaces of Europe, they are set amongst gardens well beyond the city confines.

With water at a premium, wells and reservoirs assumed great significance in a desert population's expansion. The technology for sinking deep wells was developed around the beginning of the second millennium. William Sleeman, a British official famous for suppressing the *thugs* (a murderous Hindu sect), describes the traditional method seen near Bharatpur. In 1836 he watched work on 'the well peculiar to Upper India':

> It is built up in the form of a round tower or cylindrical shell of burnt bricks, well cemented with good mortar, and covered inside and out with good stucco work, and let down by degrees, as the earth is removed by men at work digging under the light earthy or sandy foundation inside and out.
>
> In the desert where shortage of water and fuel precludes brick, wells are often lined with camel bones.

Building a well was an expensive enterprise undertaken by a wealthy merchant or baron to the greater glory of his clan. Shekhawati wells are marked by two or four tall pillars beside the shaft. Larger ones are set in a masonry platform raised three feet or more above the surrounding land. Directed by men of the Mali caste teams of bullocks haul up leather bags of water, which are spilled into a channel. This leads to bathing reservoirs sunk in the platform which drain through cattle troughs into an irrigation system.

The groundwater is often so brackish, barely drinkable, that many households construct a spectacular rainwater store, called a *koond*. The largest feasible area is smoothed over into a shallow saucer-like shape. A deep circular pit at its centre is lined with hardpan and lime mortar and over it a dome is constructed on a frame of brushwood. The saucer-like surface is plastered. Rainwater flows into the centre and drains into the pit through channels. A small hatch, set in the dome and generally padlocked, gives the owner access to sweet water which is always offered to guests and at weddings.

A *johara* enlarges on the same principle. A step-floored tank up to 50 yards square, lined with lime mortar, it is dug at the lowest point in a natural saucer of land. This requires a large labour force, often financed by wealthy merchants at times of acute famine. Many *johara* are decorative, surrounded by arches and domes on slender pillars. The terrible famine, 'Chappan Akaal', ('the famine of '56' occurred in 1899 AD, or 1956 by the Hindu calendar) came as Shekhawati *seths* were amassing huge fortunes. A number of such projects, including 'Sethani ka Johara' ('the Tank of the Wealthy Lady') near Churu, date from the period.

Above left:
In the desert, water architecture is spectacular.
The shaft of this well is set in a high platform
with four tall pillars around it. At each corner
is a little arched pavilion, constructed from
hardpan. Shekhawati, Rajasthan.

Below left:
A koond, *a saucer of masonry, drains precious
rainwater from its centre into a subterranean
reservoir beneath a domed cover. Water is
drawn from the reservoir through a lockable
trapdoor. Churu district, Rajasthan.*

Right:
A johara, *a reservoir dug at the lowest point in
a saucer of land. Monsoon water collects in a
masonry-lined tank. Joharas were sometimes
constructed by wealthy merchants as famine
relief projects, beautifully surrounded by
domes and pavilions. Churu, Rajasthan.*

Previous pages:
Chhatri *at Danta Ramgarh, Rajasthan.*

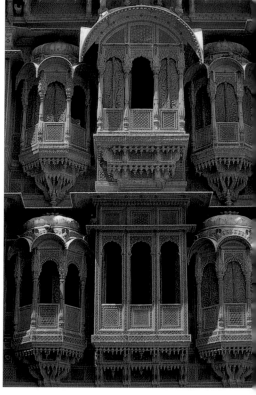

Above:
Detail of stone haveli facade. Ornate jharokhas (balconies) with wooden-shuttered openings project over the street. They are shaded by arched chhajjas (eaves) while beneath hang decorative stone pendants. Jaisalmer, Rajasthan.

Left:
A classic merchant haveli of carved sandstone. Each house is raised on a high plinth containing storage cellars. The otla or open platform bears a display of items for sale to tourists. The facade is gloriously decorated: every part of the stonework is carved, pierced by fine jalis sheltered by tiers of chhajjas. Long stone spouts carry rainwater clear of the masonry. Jaisalmer, Rajasthan.

Jaisalmer city grew up on the caravan trade between Thatta port at the mouth of the Indus, and the states of Rajasthan and the northern plains. Protected by its Rajput rulers, part of the city and the palace were within the fort walls. The local buildings drew on rich deposits of golden sandstone, both soft and resilient. The beauty of its architecture draws many tourists, resulting in less appealing modern excrescences. Jaisalmer, Rajasthan.

The merchants of Shekhawati would have preferred good building stone to brick or hardpan, but it was not easily available. A handful imported red sandstone and built heavily carved *havelis*. To the west are good stone outcrops and in the cities of Bikaner and Jodhpur, plastered and painted *havelis* give way to finely carved sandstone: still further west these are outclassed by those of Jaisalmer.

Jaisalmer sandstone is golden yellow, sometimes lensed with red. Plentiful and easily worked, it was used not only in the construction of the hilltop fort, city walls, palaces and great *havelis* but even for small houses and for paving the narrow streets. Some beds cleave to produce ideal slabs for paving stones, shelves, *chhajja* and cantilevered steps which often run up the side of a house.

The massive stone is perfect for carving, soft yet resistant to weathering. Local Muslim masons exploited it fully for such masterpieces as the Patwa and Nathmal family *havelis*. These mansions are four or five storeys high, built on a high plinth containing storerooms, with several *choubara* (small rooms) on the roof. A single courtyard runs up through the house, the private, family, area. Large rooms at the front of the ground floor and the *otla* (open platform) or verandah form the semi-private area for visitors.

The rear and side walls of a house, if not adjoining busy streets, are of plain ashlar penetrated above ground floor level by *jali* windows. The facades are glorious, a cascade of finely worked stone. *Jharokhas* (balconies), rectangular or semioctagonal in plan, their side panels rich with relief work of flowers, extend over the street. From them hang ranks of carved golden stalactites. They are screened from public view by a lacework of *jali* penetrated by the occasional tiny window, notable for its remarkably plain wooden shutter. Above each window is an arched canopy, its delicate corners descending in slender points. Wherever possible stone is carved into abstract, vegetal or figurative forms, with even such innovations as railway trains appearing. Long stone spouts carry rainwater well clear of all this delicate stonework.

Each door surround is beautifully crafted. The brass-inlaid wooden shutters open into a porch where a direct view of the courtyard is denied by a screen wall through which a little *jali* peers. The rooms are small, restricted by the length of stone slabs or roughly shaped wooden joists used for the ceiling. A cornice projects from the top of the wall on which the joist ends lie, slightly reducing the span required. In the most luxurious houses imported wooden planks are used for some ceilings.

The mansion of Salim Singh, a Jain merchant, and all-powerful minister to the Maharawal from the 1790s until 1824, is unique. Beside the customary courtyard a great shaft of masonry rises, crowned by an intricately carved chamber cantilevered out on all sides. No mean feat of engineering, this structure survived until 1993 when, as a result of heavy monsoon rains, nine of its thirty-eight domed balconies fell. Now despoiled, the interior was richly embellished with gold, indigo, mirrorwork, deep blue glass flasks and little glass paintings.

Within the walls of the hilltop citadel are more carved houses. There are also smaller mud dwellings built by fort guards, their form and white painted decoration relating to their homes in surrounding villages. They have no courtyards, sharing the cul-de-sac in front for this purpose.

Above:
In western Rajasthani towns wood is in short supply and is confined to shutters and door surrounds. Door shutters are reinforced with brass or iron, as is the threshold, prone to heavy wear. The door can be locked with a chain looping over a rung set in the lintel or, as here, the sill. Jaisalmer, Rajasthan.

Left:
Where stone cleaves into thin slabs it is often used to create cantilevered flight of steps, one end of the slab set deep into the masonry of the wall. This method is commonly used for external stairways in western Rajasthan.

CHAPTER FIVE

Towards
The Arabian Sea

*Gujarat, Daman
and Diu*

A RANGE OF POOR HILLS separates Gujarat state from Rajasthan. To the south rainfall is higher, sustaining richer vegetation on better agricultural land, coupled with very different geological resources. Like Rajasthan, much of Gujarat was divided amongst princes, mainly Rajputs. Their reign between the eleventh and fourteenth centuries saw the construction of some magnificent temples, *vav* (step-wells) and reservoirs. The Hindu princes were overthrown by Muslims and a sultanate of Gujarat was founded in 1403. Inspired by existing buildings, the new rulers developed their own style of architecture, using local Hindu forms in the construction of Muslim mosques and tombs. Ahmedabad, set up as capital by Ahmed Shah in 1411, is rich in Gujarati monumental and vernacular domestic buildings.

The Sultanate gave way to Mughal rule in the late sixteenth century and that in turn was eclipsed by Hindu Marathas during the eighteenth century. All three eras influenced Gujarati architecture. The Maratha Gaekwad clan held much of Gujarat, their leader, the Maharaja of Baroda, becoming the most senior ruler in the state. During the early nineteenth century the British extended direct or indirect control over the whole state.

Gujarat's mixed populace includes a large tribal element of Kolis and Bhils, still a dominant part of the population of the eastern part of the state. Prior to the rise of Calcutta and Bombay the most important port of northern India was Surat, north of Bombay on the Gujarat coast. Trade has long been an important Gujarati occupation. Although most of the merchants are Hindu there are important Muslim business communities, including Bohras, and there are the Parsis, Persian followers of Zarathustra who fled before Islam in the eighth century.

Parts of the state, the second richest in India, are agriculturally fertile. On the coast many fishermen become sailors. A maritime tradition gave rise to an eighteenth-century urge to explore. Tradition claims that the ruler of Kutch sent one of his vessels as far as Holland.

Throughout India towns are divided into sectors, each dominated by one caste and trade. This reflects a rural pattern where each village is controlled by one caste which holds the land. In urban Gujarat, housing was often arranged in *pols*, each consisting of one or several streets inhabited by people of the same caste. The *pol* is a semi-private area entered by a single gateway where a *chowkidar* (watchman) used to regulate access. It was once virtually self-sufficient, having its own well and a staff of workers living just outside to service it. These ranged from jewellers and drapers, through vendors of milk and food to sweepers who emptied the lavatories.

The organizational system has gone, but many *pols* remain. The entrance gate was shared by the inhabitants and certain of the services were common responsibility. Such a lifestyle required a group to control funds contributed by residents towards its upkeep. Money for communal expenses was raised partly by fines levied by the *pol* council and by a small percentage on the sale price of every house. The individual's house was his own responsibility but there was control over its ownership and an owner could not sell without consulting the council.

While Rajasthani merchants excelled in their stone mansions those of Gujarat built no less impressively in wood. In the north and east massive teak beams were used to construct half-timbered *havelis*. These buildings evolved from local timber resources but during the nineteenth century, as the forests fell, teak was brought from the Western Ghats, especially from the Dangs district. It was also imported by sea from the Malabar coast (Kerala) and even from Burma.

The best examples of the full-framed northern Gujarati house form are concentrated in the cities of Ahmedabad and Baroda and in smaller towns of Kheda and Mehsana districts. The builders were successful businessmen, usually Hindu Banias (merchants) but also Muslims, particularly of the Bohra community, and Parsis.

Variations in the layout of urban wood-framed houses are attributed to local rural domestic forms from which they descended. Tradition also intervenes, dictating, for example, that a house's side walls should not be exactly parallel but must diverge slightly, making the rear marginally wider than the front.

Northern Gujarati urban houses enclose a courtyard but, unlike the *chauk* of a North Indian *haveli*, this is a space-divider rather than the building's heart. For a Hindu merchant the front section of his house was a business office or shop. It was therefore a semi-private area in an urban context lacking permanent markets and bazaars seen elsewhere in India. This front invariably has an open platform, or *otlo*, where the family (today, more often women than men) can sit in the evening to gossip and socialize with their neighbours. Sometimes sheltered by a verandah, but often little more than a shelf beside the street, it encourages informal meeting.

The section of street in front of a house can be taken over on special occasions as an extension of the householder's domain. Here, blocking the street, he erects a colourful *shamiana* (tent) to entertain guests for a daughter's marriage or a religious ceremony.

Known as a *khadki*, the section of house in front of the courtyard is also semi-private. There could be little discrimination as to who could enter to do business. The stairs leading up from the *otlo* are not enclosed in a stairwell. In most Gujarati houses stairs consist merely of a ladder-like flight of flat wooden treads, a dangling rope or low handrail providing support. A sliding panel or hinged door surrounded by a low balustrade on the floor above can seal off the upper room. The stairs lead up to a first floor *diwankhana*, the most richly decorated and well lit room in the house. This is for display, the scene for formal business and entertainment. Its windows are often colour-glazed and in rich *havelis* there may be old Belgian chandeliers and glass lamps. It contains the best furniture, usually Western-style tables and chairs. In the *diwankhana* and on the facade outside is some of the finest carving in the house. The motifs are mostly geometric or plant-based, but some are figurative. The animals depicted totally ignore scriptural injunctions and include many beasts proscribed for domestic housing whilst neglecting some that are deemed propitious. A house, according to the classic texts, should not be decorated with carved gods, demons, stars, *nagas* (serpent spirits), *apsaras* (angels) or elephants, horses and lions. Amongst the permitted figures were Lakshmi, Gauri, flowers, parrots and partridges. This further indicates that scriptures related to housing were more an intellectual exercize, healthily ignored, than constraining regulations.

The entrance is turned into a feature, the door surround being finely carved. A characteristic element of Gujarat joinery is a *tolla*, otherwise seen only in medieval Abyssinian stone architecture. The door frame is in two parts. The outer frame actually holds the shutters and supports the section of wall above it.

Verandah in the courtyard of a Bohra Muslim haveli. The swing-seat and wooden pillars set in stone bases are traditional Gujarati features. In the background, prized china is displayed on shelves arranged in three rows of three, just as in the room traditionally used by Muslims for this purpose, the chini khana. *A drain in the corner of the courtyard funnels rainwater into an underground cistern. Patan, Mahesana district, Gujarat.*

The kitchen of a Muslim haveli *in Patan. The display of pots and pans is characteristically Gujarati.*

The doors open against the inner frame. The wall above is set in a pair of *tollas*, one at either end of the lintel. A *tolla*, H-shaped, holds the two sections together. It shows as a corbel-like boss at the angle of the frame. At the bottom the two frames are secured in a massive wooden threshold. The same structure appears in some window frames. Sometimes there is a double *tolla*, with a pair at the bottom as well as the top of the frame.

The rear door of the *khadki* section divides it from the private interior. The courtyard acts as a forecourt separating the *khadki* from the inner core. Usually only two rooms open onto it: the kitchen (so that smoke from the hearth can easily escape) and a *paniaru* (water store). Both, by tradition, are situated on the left side. Gujarati women make their kitchen an area for display despite the fact that, for orthodox Hindus, access to it is restricted. Cooking vessels of brass, copper (preferred by Muslims) and steel, daily polished, are arranged in order of size along a series of shelves. The water store often contains a small well in addition to water pots. In the congested cities this was liable to pollution from the neighbours' drainage soakaways. To counter this, many houses have a *tanku*, rainwater cistern, under the courtyard, plaster-lined to protect it from seepage. Any rainwater drains from the roof into the *tanku*, perhaps explaining another tradition: the *mobh* (ridge) of a tiled roof, parallel to the facade, is always set asymmetrically, towards the rear of house. This causes more rainwater to be deflected into the *tanku*, less into the street.

The courtyard still functions as a space for dry-weather household chores such as washing clothes and vessels, preparing grain and vegetables and as a bathing area for women. In Hindu Gujarati houses the roof is usually pitched and tiled, denying the

Right:
A ground-floor window with interwoven metal rods set in a strong wooden frame forming a defensive jali. *The projecting bosses at either side of the lintel are* tollas, *linking an inner frame to the visible one. Ghogha, Bhavnagar district.*

Far right:
Detail of the capital of a teak pillar. The timbers of Gujarati merchant houses are richly carved with decorative designs.

Perhaps one of the finest examples of stone jali-work to be found anywhere, a glorious carved tree of life forms the window design for Sid Sayyid's mosque in Ahmedabad.

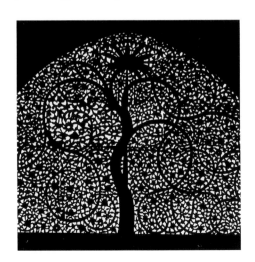

family a terrace on which to sleep in summer. Men avoid the heat by sleeping in the courtyard. Women use the *reveshi*, a room open onto the courtyard. Beyond this is the *parsal*, a room which functions as the eating place and where women sleep in cold weather. Here the characteristic Gujarati *hinchko*, swing-seat, is suspended on chains from the central beam. In a warm and humid climate the gentle motion of the swing creates a breeze with minimal effort, quite apart from its restful motion.

The rearmost space is known as the *ordo* (literally 'room'). In a rural house this is usually a single room but in the urban context it is often subdivided. Reserved for women, this is the most private part of the house. Here goods are stored, grain held in great clay jars, built either by women of the house or by a potter employed for the purpose. Everyday clothes are kept on lathe-turned wooden pegs fixed in the walls. Best clothes and other more valuable items are stored in a *patara*, a large wooden chest on wheels, essential part of a Gujarati bride's dowry. Jewelry, gold, silver and cash is concealed in secret niches both in the *patara* and in the fabric of the building.

One room is set aside to confine women during their two states of 'impurity' – menstruation and after giving birth. Throughout the world, many societies deem women unclean in either state. Since the woman is not allowed out of this room a covered soakaway latrine is set in the floor.

The woodwork of the facade, and indeed of any surface open to public gaze, is covered with fine carving. The upper facade of buildings in Ahmedabad and Mehsana district is made of wooden panelling like that found in Turkey and other parts of western Asia. It is heavily carved with repetitive relief patterns, both geometric and floral, reminiscent of the wooden cloth-printing blocks turned out at nearby Pethapur. Probably the same workforce did both jobs.

Above:
A lively carved first-floor facade weighs heavily on its supporting beam. A large expanse of window illuminates and ventilates the upper room when the shutters are open. The bottom section of the window has metal railings to prevent the unwary from falling. Ahmedabad.

Left:
A small, beautifully carved urban house. A pulley under the eaves allows the occupant to draw up supplies and water from the front door. The panelling on either side of the window is carved with a repetitive motif similar to blocks produced by cloth printers in nearby Pethapur. The double door is characteristic. In hot weather the solid leaves can be left open, the barred ones closed so that security can be combined with good ventilation. Ahmedabad.

Right:
Deeply carved struts supporting a projecting upper storey are particularly striking on Gujarati facades. Often they combine struggling animals with entwining plant designs. Ahmedabad.

Below:
A typical Gujarati urban frontage. Above the gutter rises a high plinth of a verandah sheltered by a projecting floor sustained by carved struts and wooden pillars set in stone bases. In the congested urban setting this verandah extends the living area. Windows are firmly sealed with metal jalis. Ahmedabad.

Labour-intensive and demanding increasingly expensive timber, as the twentieth century advanced Gujarati wooden *havelis* have ceased to be viable. Towns like Sankheda thrived on producing carved woodwork for these *havelis*, such as gloriously sinister figurative struts, and found demand slacking as prices rose. The craftsmen diversified, turning to lathe-turned lacquered work, furniture and household items, which now completely eclipse carved architectural elements.

Peace and stability in the nineteenth century provided an ideal environment for display by a mercantile community which had so benefited from it. This was the great period of conspicuous domestic building. Decoration did not end with wood carving: the nineteenth century was one of the richest periods of mural painting the country has known. Plasterwork (and, to a lesser degree, woodwork) was painted both indoors and out. Most of the painting has faded or fallen with the plaster, but some remains. Typical of Gujarati mural decoration, seen in Ahmedabad, in Kheda district and west to Kutch, is a painted gable-end showing a tiger posed on either side of a central circular medallion. In Kheda district particularly, the facades of houses and temples often retain a large number of both secular and religious pictures, many clearly dating from the twentieth century. The largest *havelis* boast finer work in their display rooms. Even modest nineteenth-century businessmen could run to a little religious decoration. A room in Mahatma Gandhi's family house in Porbandar has a series of panels showing the ten incarnations of Vishnu, preserved when the house was turned into a museum to the Father of the Nation. Today, mural painting flourishes in *haveli*-temples, often dedicated to the popular Swami Narayan cult. The new generation of religious pictures are in bright acrylics.

Three techniques of timber-masonry construction were used in Gujarat. The first, timber bonding, resembles the method employed in Kashmir and Himachal Pradesh where baulks of timber are integrated into the wall structure at intervals. This is seen in northern Gujarat and Saurashtra. More common in the north is a second technique, half-timbering, where horizontals are coupled with vertical timber columns to bear the load. Domestic architecture from Surat southwards employs a third technique, full framing. Here vertical pillars are linked by beams in a single direction, making a frame capable of standing independent of its masonry walls. The plan differs from that elsewhere in Gujarat, lacking a courtyard, which is replaced by a walled yard at the rear. This transforms the organization of the building, requiring a back door, thus neutralizing the progressive advance into the darker, more secret, interior of the dwelling.

In north and south Gujarat urban houses are generally constructed in rows along *pol* streets. Those of Saurashtra are usually free-standing, based on a rather different plan. The larger rural houses, such as those of the agricultural Kathi caste, resemble those of Jats in Rajasthan and elsewhere, a gatehouse giving onto a compound, the forecourt. This structure is called a *delo*. Saurashtran urban housing takes on this concept along with the name.

In Ghogha, an ancient port near Bhavnagar left high and dry by a retreating sea, some traditional housing survives. Again, a semi-private section of the house – in this case the *delo* – is separated from the private area by a courtyard to which the kitchen and water store are adjoined. Often positioned to face the rising sun, the

A Parsi merchant mansion in Diu is built from the local soft yellow limestone. The lower windows with carved projecting lintels are typical of this part of Gujarat. An otlo (raised plinth for sitting) runs along the facade; there is a sheltered sitting area inside the covered porch. The plasterwork was initially painted with floral designs. The upper balconied windows owe much to the Portuguese who ruled here for almost 450 years. Parsiwada, Diu.

delo may be further estranged from the private quarters by setting it at right angles to the facade of the dwelling. Stairs up to the *diwankhana* ascend from the courtyard rather than the roadside *otlo*.

Ghogha's houses are timber-bonded, built of stone fragments or brick with shaped stone quoins. Walls are consolidated with mud mortar, the brickwork pointed and covered with lime plaster. Ceilings consist of a frame of timber beams and rafters supporting stone or terracotta tiles some 2½ inches thick. Over these is an 8-inch layer of coarse gravel laid in lime plaster or mud. If it is to be the floor of a room, the final layer is mud and dung plaster; the roof is finished in waterproof lime plaster. Internal walls are plaster with mud and dung but are also sometimes panelled with wooden planks.

Often adjoining a Hindu or Jain *haveli*, or within a *pol*, stands a *chabutra*. A free-standing pigeon loft, it is built to encourage the birds purely in recognition of their auspicious nature. Generally it is a little wooden roofed structure supported on a single pillar. This is incised with *gokhla*, special grooves which can act as niches for candles or oil lamps to illuminate it for special occasions. Some *chabutra* are considerable masonry towers, veritable pigeon condominiums.

Muslim communities such as the Bohras and Sodagars of Patan build houses modified from the Hindu plan. The Bohra community, an unorthodox clan of converts from Hinduism, are usually involved in business. Unlike the Hindus, their shop or office is quite separate from the home; one is in the commercial part of town, the other in a 'ghetto', or *bohrawad*, inside the old walled town but cut off from other communities. A *bohrawad* is entered by several gates, often passing beneath buildings, and was once sealed and guarded at night. Within its confines, along the wandering alleys linking it, is a mosque, community hall and the priest's house.

As with most merchant communities, the late nineteenth and early twentieth centuries saw a period of conspicuous building as 'pax britannica' brought prosperity. The Bohras followed contemporary fashion, imitating elements of architecture and furnishing from those of the ruling power. Peace rendered town walls redundant and, as they were demolished, there was room to expand. Richer members of the community sometimes established a grid-plan sector of the *bohrawad* alongside its old core. A fine example of a later *bohrawad* is that of Siddhpur, 65 miles north of Ahmedabad.

A traditional Bohra house diverges from that of a Hindu merchant in being a true courtyard dwelling. The entrance owes its origin to the Saurashtran *delo*, retaining the name *dehli*. Muslims, especially groups like Sodagars, and to a lesser extent the Bohras, are stricter about *purdah* (the concealment of women) than Hindus, attempting to hide the *zenana* or women's section of the house from visitors. This more enclosed attitude probably explains why the *otlo* (street-side platform) is little-used by Muslim householders. The main entrance gives onto a lobby which is isolated from the private courtyard by a wooden screen. In some houses there are two courtyards, the smaller being intended for guests. The courtyard walls are often brightly painted with *chini khana* (display shelves) set in the walls, often arranged in three rows of three, a traditional Islamic layout known as *navkhand*. These are used to display attractive items of porcelain or other family treasures. Such sets of shelves were a Mughal innovation.

Characteristic of many Muslim houses in Patan is a *vavdan* (wind catcher) intended to direct the prevailing breeze down into the house. It consists of a vertical projection, L-shaped in plan, oriented so that the centre of its right angle faces southwest, towards the prevailing summer wind. Within the fabric of the house the L becomes a square shaft opening through the wall of a room, often the dark, airless *ordo*. A wooden shutter made it possible to close this opening. Today, in an era of electric fans, this is neglected and the sloping roof which deflected the wind down the shaft is usually absent. The best functional examples of these wind catchers in the subcontinent are seen in Sind (southern Pakistan). There are other vertical ventilating shafts in these Bohra houses which lack any projection above roof level but merely encourage the air to circulate.

Traditional temples in Gujarat follow two forms. Most widespread are variations on the northern Indian style, a *sikhara* towering above the *garbha griha* and a rectangular or cruciform *mandapa* where the faithful can greet the deity. There is, however, a vernacular style which, like that of Rajasthan, is an adaptation of the local *haveli*. Such *haveli*-temples lack a *sikhara* and enclose one or more courtyards. The shrine usually faces east out of an arched chamber giving onto the inner courtyard.

The island of Diu, just off the Saurashtran coast, was held by the Portuguese from the early sixteenth century until 1961. They had been granted the right to the fort in return for sending infantry troops to the Sultan of Gujarat to hold back the Mughals. From there they took over the rest of the little island. The troops never arrived at Ahmedabad. The Mughals, however, did. As elsewhere in Gujarat, Diu town is divided into *wadas*, sectors based on caste or religious affiliation. There is a

An intricate little cusped niche set into the courtyard wall is intended to display family porcelain. Bohra haveli, *Patan, Mehsana district.*

Following pages:
Like the Rajasthanis, the Gujaratis developed a vernacular form of temple based on the merchant haveli. *Heavily decorated and brightly painted, they are often dedicated, as is this one in Ahmedabad, to the teacher Swami Narayan. Stucco and carved wooden decoration shows a guard on either side of the door, reclining Vishnu above it and a series of Vishnu incarnations carved on the leaves of the door.*

The lintel of the main entrance to a house often bears some auspicious motif at its centre.

Top: A purnakalasha, *overflowing pot, popular on Hindu lintels in Gujarat, represents Lakshmi, Goddess of Wealth.*

Middle: The figure of a Jain tirthankar *(teacher) from the lintel of a Jain temple.*

Bottom: The lintel of a Parsi house bears a plant in a pot, probably a variation on the purnakalasha.

Right:
The Parsis came from Persia in the eighth century, bringing the tradition of exposing the dead for scavenging birds. For this they built Towers of Silence, with a screen wall hiding the corpses laid out on the platform. Later the bones are put in the central pit. Fudam, Diu.

Parsiwada near the port where the mercantile Parsi community built some handsome houses and a temple. Ferenghiwada, to the east, close to the impressive Iberian churches, housed the *ferenghi* (foreign) community.

More than four centuries of Portuguese rule and intermarriage touched traditional architecture. Here, houses represent a more southern European concept. The internal courtyard is very small or absent and the building spreads upwards rather than outwards in this compact town. Diu is provided with plentiful, soft yet resilient shelly limestone of a pleasant yellow. The landscape outside the impressive sixteenth-century town wall is pitted with deep quarries from which ashlar blocks for fortification and housing were dug. Much of the timber required for beams and rafters, however, was brought in from the mainland. Any combination of materials has inherent weaknesses which eventually contrive to make the house uninhabitable. In Diu, as in many other parts of India, this is the vulnerability of wooden elements to decay and the depredations of termites. Timber pillars are usually set in a stone base to protect them. These are flat-roofed houses, whose beams and joists support a considerable weight of stone tile and waterproof mortar. Progressive rotting of the woodwork brings the roof down.

Hindu and Parsi houses in Diu are built with a much used *otlo* where the family sit in the evening. In common with many houses in Gujarati coastal areas the front door consists of outer and inner leaves. The outer pair are merely light frames housing ranks of metal bars. The inner pair are of solid wood, capable of being firmly bolted outside and in. In daytime the inner door can be left open, the outer

closed, allowing air to circulate freely but restricting access. The same is true of many of the windows. The centre of the lintel generally bears a carved religious motif, a blessing on the occupants and their visitors. The figure of Ganesh, the Lord of Beginnings, who blesses so many Hindu entrances, is ubiquitous on Rajasthani lintels but in Gujarat and Diu he is often displaced by an overflowing pot. This is an ancient Hindu symbol representing Lakshmi, goddess of wealth. Muslim lintels are blank or bear the name of Allah whilst the Christians of Bassein (Maharashtra) choose a heart and cross motif.

Above both door and windows in Diu, as in Saurashtra and Kutch, heavily carved stonework projects to shelter the doorway. This feature is continued down the sides of the doorway to include a little lamp niche on either side of the door. There are similar niches, independent of the lintel, on either side of the windows to hold little lamps on the night of Diwali, 'festival of light', in October or November. The soft stone was also carved to decorate buildings in other parts of Saurashtra with figurative sculpture, following a style seen occasionally in the local murals. The figure of a Parsi notable on the jetty at Diu is a good example of such turn-of-century work; others line the walls of a *dharamshala* in nearby Una.

The porous ashlar of the houses is protected by a layer of lime plaster. In Diu this was often decorated with bright painting, architectural forms such as rows of false balusters being added to geometric and plant patterns. Some of the houses are painted with ochre wash, reminiscent of Iberian colours from which the fashion descended.

The facade of the typical Diu house mixes Iberian features with truly Gujarati ones. High up on the wall there are T-shaped holes intended for parrots and sparrows to nest in. The window shutters are usually in three sections. The bottom is made up of closely spaced vertical wooden bars fashioned to hold little rectangles of translucent shell. This form of glazing seems to have come in with the Portuguese and is seen in all their Indian enclaves. In front of this section there is often a wrought iron railing to prevent children from falling. Above this is a pair of glazed shutters. The topmost section is a glazed flap opening upwards and outwards. Together, these allow the occupants to regulate the flow of air in a region where a continual sea breeze makes fans redundant. Above windows and doors are ventilators, usually round or oval, with carved stone surrounds. Between the first-floor windows is a pot containing a growing plant of *tulsi*, the sacred basil. An open balcony, usually of stone supported by brackets but occasionally of carved wood, is again more Iberian than Indian.

Inside the door the first room is used to entertain guests and contains a swing-seat. From here, open stairs, ladder-like, run to the upper floors, eventually emerging on the roof under cover of a little tiled shelter. The back rooms are reserved for privacy. Rainwater cisterns have an increased significance in this coastal region of porous rock since many wells give brackish, barely drinkable water.

The wells and tanks of Gujarat are less striking than those of Rajasthani regions such as Shekhawati except when they reach monumental stature. Hindu memorial *chhatris* are less common here, usually confined to royalty. Certain communities, particularly Rajputs and Bhil tribals, erect steles known as *palliya* to their dead.

These initially commemorated men who died in battle in defence of their village or its cattle. They are carved with a relief of an armed horseman. Sun and moon symbols at either side are said to indicate that the man will be remembered as long as the sun and moon remain. Others display a carved hand and arm, celebrating a faithful widow who committed *sati* on her husband's pyre. *Palliya* are now rarely erected to Rajputs but the Bhil tradition continues and the deceased's life is annually celebrated by a family party at the memorial and its repainting.

Parsis, Zoroastrians fleeing before the tide of Islam, landed in Diu in the early eighth century, shifting later to Eastern Gujarat. Their traditions so respect the elements that it is not permitted to defile earth, fire or water with the dead. They build special towers in which corpses are exposed, to be devoured by vultures and crows. These towers are an essential feature of Parsi settlements but, like their fire temples, are closed to outsiders. The Parsis left Diu when the Indian Army took the island in 1961, but their Towers of Silence remain, pill-box shaped and only some twelve feet high. In the interior, there is a circular central pit surrounded by a wide shelf which gently slopes towards it. This shelf is divided into shallow sunken sections, each shaped to hold a corpse, small ones near the entrance being designed for children. A high wall completing the 'pill-box' conceals the interior.

The coast is a long stretch of flat *kikar* (a thorny acacia bush) and palm-lined beach, sandy at its western end but increasingly muddy eastwards, towards the mouths of several large rivers. It is punctuated by fishing villages, often situated in the estuary of some little creek, offering shelter to larger vessels during the monsoon. The fishing settlements consist of single-storeyed, tile-roofed houses. Individual houses are generally arranged in rows, often terraced, each having a covered verandah with a low wall or a bench to serve as an *otlo*. On the west-facing coast of southern Gujarat, where the monsoon is heavy, a large verandah is essential as a working space during the days of downpour. Walls are made of a roughly shaped wooden frame covered with bamboo or palm leaf, and plastered with a mud and dung mixture. The roof is either thatched with palm fronds or, an indication of greater affluence, tiled. The great mud jars which serve as grain stores are constructed just inside the door, in the area that is used to entertain visitors. The kitchen and water store are at the back of the house. Beyond them is a second, narrower verandah giving onto a small compound. The remaining space can be adapted for use as required, with one or two private bedrooms partitioned off.

During the monsoon months of June to September, when the seas are too rough for fishing, men work on maintenance of nets and boats as well as agriculture. They survive these lean months on dried fish and home-grown vegetables. For the rest of the year the men are away fishing for long periods, putting out from distant ports. Many join the national or merchant navy, which keeps them away for even longer periods. This results in a close-knit community ready to support the single-parent families.

CHAPTER SIX

*Maharashtra,
eastern Gujarat,
Madhya Pradesh,
western Orissa*

THE TRIBAL HEARTLAND

CENTRAL INDIA comprises the north and central Deccan plateau along with the Ghats, the slopes leading down to the coastal plain, which fringe the Deccan to the east and west. A swathe of upland, the area includes Maharashtra, eastern Gujarat, Madhya Pradesh, India's largest state, and the jungles of western Orissa. There are rich agricultural lands producing sugar and cotton, but much of the landscape is hilly, its poor soil supporting sparse, dry jungle. Into such impoverished, easily defensible terrain, earlier inhabitants retreated, as new, dynamic waves of invaders advanced to seize the fertile plains. So this became the tribal belt, with a concentration of older peoples ranging from the Bhils of eastern Gujarat and western Madhya Pradesh, through the food-gathering Gonds and iron-working Agaria of Bastar in southeast Madhya Pradesh, to the Saora and Juang of Orissa. They built small settlements of mud-and-thatch huts and, prior to Independence, were generally subservient to some non-tribal ruler, a Hindu Rajput or a Muslim nawab.

Central India is home to many *adivasi* (pre-Aryan) communities strongly influenced by Hinduism but preserving their own rituals and deities. These have often left an imprint on local Hindu practice. The great Jagannath trinity of the temple at Puri is descended as much from *adivasi* ancestors as from Krishna and his siblings, whom they nominally represent. *Adivasi* tribal social organization and traditions differ markedly from those of the neighbouring caste Hindus. The sexes are far more integrated in tribal society and women have a considerable amount of freedom, a characteristic exploited by Hindu youth. Each community developed its own form of settlement and housing, the product of environment, available materials and lifestyle.

Themselves free from caste taboos, tribals are beyond the Pale for orthodox Hindus. But their position is sometimes ambiguous. For instance, by tradition a Bhil must apply the *tilak* mark (in this case the equivalent of coronation) to the forehead of a new Maharana of Udaipur, head of the Sisodia clan, the seniormost Hindu royalty in India.

Two major groups, Rathwa and Chodhri, constitute the most important tribal element in the hills of eastern Gujarat and western Madhya Pradesh. Their houses are of wattle and daub, roofed with thatch or tile. When starting a house Chodhris perform a special *puja* – religious ceremony – focused on one of the wooden pillars. A hole is dug where it is to be erected and a foundation layer of crushed brick is put in to protect the wood. Onto this, rice, red *kumkum* powder, flowers and some money are placed. Prayers are directed towards Ganesh, the Hindu deity of auspicious beginnings. Red marks are applied with two fingers to the pillar which is then garlanded with a string of mango leaves. With the post in place more broken brick is stuffed down the hole on all sides to hold it upright. It is also usual amongst the Chodhris to follow certain rituals propitiating the dead before embarking on construction.

This ritual complete, the builder can start on the basic frame, which consists of a line of three axial posts, two rows of three pillars arranged parallel to it on either side. Those along the axis do not extend the whole height of the building but support a long beam. Five short uprights set on this support a ridge pole.

The Chodhris avoid building houses facing eastwards: this direction is reserved for temples. Nails are not used. The top of each upright is shaped so that a peg projects from its centre. This fits into a socket in the bottom of the *kumbhi* or capital, in the top of which a hollow is scooped out. A beam fits snugly into this hollow. Proportions are fixed: if the central row of posts supporting the ridge is 9 feet high then the distance between these and the neighbouring rows on either side is also 9 feet. The outer row is half this measurement (i.e., 4 feet 6 inches) in height. The facade is parallel with the ridge, and the front section, between the outer and second row of posts, acts as a covered verandah. The floor is raised on a 6- to 8-inch-high earthen plinth to avoid flooding during the heavy monsoon.

When the basic frame is complete, another Ganesh *puja* is performed, a coin slipped between two wooden elements, a swastika mark applied to the ridge beam

Tribal settlements are generally found in the less fertile, hilly regions. The mud and rubble walls of these low houses are rarely broken by ventilation openings. The thatched roof shelters a verandah, an extension of the working area. Raised platforms adjoining the house are recognized as semi-private. Kurli, Orissa.

and mango leaves suspended from it. Vermilion, rice and flowers are placed in a white cloth and this package, along with a coconut, is also hung from the beam. The roof may be two- or four-sloped. Traditionally the roof was covered with locally made rounded tiles, fired by the potter caste, but these need renewing every 3 to 4 years and, being heavy, require a strong timber frame. They are generally replaced by lighter factory-produced ones, known as 'Mangalori' (from Mangalore, Karnataka) or *angrezi* (English) tiles.

The houses of the poorer folk, however, are thatched with straw covered with great teak leaves. This may be cheaper but it requires annual attention, especially where monsoon rainfall is high. Walls are made of woven split-bamboo sections, often bought from the Kotwadia caste whose occupation includes weaving baskets. They are plastered over with mud mixed with finely chopped paddy straw. When the surface has dried it is given a final plaster of cow dung. Sections of the wall, loosely woven and left unplastered, function as windows, allowing light to penetrate the gloom.

Most Chodhri houses have two basic rooms: a large one takes up two thirds of the internal area. One end of this is cordoned off for the animals at night, and at the other end the family spread out their mats to sleep. There is a hollow in the floor,

A tribal village outside Puri backs onto a pond. Under a state-sponsored initiative, ponds have recently been stocked with fast-growing fish, which serve the dual function of eating mosquito larvae and providing extra protein in the villagers' diet.

not far from the door, where rice is pounded, and against the wall is a wooden stand for water pots.

A *machan* stands in front of the house, a rudimentary structure consisting of four or six uprights supporting a flat roof of poles or bamboo on which grass is loosely placed. It is used as a shelter and a shaded area where outdoor work can take place.

A common theft involves taking cattle at night. Raiders dig a tunnel under the wall and enter the sleeping house. One man fastens a rope around a buffalo's neck whilst another goads it from behind, forcing it out through the hole. If the inhabitants wake they are often too scared to intervene.

The remaining room contains the cooking hearth and grain stores, cylinders of bamboo matting lined with dung and mud. They stand some 4 feet high and are about 3 feet in diameter. The bottom is lined with large teak leaves before rice is poured in. The store is sealed and on top of it is a little cone-topped container some 18 inches in diameter, shrine of the tribe's guardian goddess, Kansari.

The gable ends may either be walled right up to the ridge, or they may be left open or partially closed by loosely hung coconut fronds. This way the space below the roof becomes a well ventilated attic. The ceiling is made of bamboo wattle, coated above and below with cow-dung plaster. The door is of bamboo wattle set on a wooden frame, extended vertically at one end to fit into sockets in both beam and floor, allowing it to pivot.

The Warlis are a small tribal group inhabiting the coastal plain and *ghats* (scarp slope) of southern Gujarat and northern Maharashtra. Their houses are notable more for decoration than structure. East-facing, the house is built amongst their fields on an earth plinth, square in plan, with a framework of wood and bamboo. This is enclosed with woven bamboo or reed walls over which mud and dung plaster is applied. The roof is thatched either with straw or great dry teak leaves, often both together. Decoration is part of the preparation for weddings or festivals, particularly that dedicated to the goddess Gauri. Using white rice paste, women of the

Above left:
The walled compound serves the function of the courtyard of an urban house. Mud-walled outhouses give onto the compound and elsewhere wattle forms the barrier. Beaten cooking-oil cans provide panels for the gate.

Above right:
The compound walls are here protected from rain erosion by large, roughly-shaped slates. They also serve to shelter drying clothes.

Stone relief on memorial chhatri. *Rotating figurative motifs are popular Hindu decorative forms. Sometimes the action takes on a meaning, as with these wrestlers throwing one another. Sometimes it is merely an odd visual device.*

Following pages
Left:
Low paddy-thatched houses form a village street, in a clearing among coconut plantations. Bhatpur village

Above right:
The wide common space between two facing rows of houses is graced by a new pump. A recent government drive to establish such pumps throughout rural India has vastly improved the quality of water supply. The gutter drains away from the pump.

Below right:
The gable end of mud houses is often protected by hanging coconut fronds. These not only deflect rain from the mud plaster but also provide increased insulation. Mukundapur, Orissa.

household cover the walls of the verandah and some external walls with meticulous murals. A mass of tiny figures dancing, farming and hunting, the paintings are votive, creating an auspicious environment for the family. As in many tribal societies the hearth has a special religious significance and conical baskets suspended from rafters above it house the family deity and ancestral spirits.

In northeast Maharashtra live a tribe of primitive agriculturists known as the Kumbi Tural. Their houses are in part double-storeyed, with strong walls of stone mortared and plastered with mud. The central core bears the second storey, surrounded on all sides by a single-storeyed section, an enclosed verandah. Roofing is a combination of local tile and grass thatch and doors are made either of wood planks or loosely woven slats of bamboo.

In Madhya Pradesh tribal folk form an important part of the population. Bastar district, a tongue of dry jungle projecting southwards into Andhra Pradesh from the southeast corner of the state, is inhabited by some of the more primitive tribal communities, including Baigra, Gond and Maria. Their architecture is remarkable more for occasional detail than for its structure or layout. Houses generally consist of one or two rooms, walled with wattle and daub and roofed in thatch or tile. Some communities, especially the Maria, carve woodwork with powerful motifs, some auspicious, others potent deterrents to the forces of evil. The communal architecture is more impressive. The Maria build open-sided temples to their deities. The temple is set in a fenced compound, with its gateway made a prominent feature. A mud wall some 18 inches high encloses the sacred space which is covered by a two-sloped roof supported on pillars made of timber or of natural stone slabs. The roof is tiled either with terracotta or unshaped slabs of stone, each drilled and lashed to the structure. This stone alternative is far heavier and requires a substantial supporting framework. Housed within are carved wooden figures and beams are shaped into animal heads at either end. A fine example of such a temple is that of Maolimata in Matnar village, not far from the much visited Chitrakuta waterfall.

Some Bastar tribals build large processional *raths* which, despite their solid wooden wheels, are more temples than vehicles. A *rath* may be twenty feet high and consists of a wheeled platform acting as base for a structure of timber cross-pieces raising the 'temple' floor some ten feet above ground level. Sheltering the image is a four-sloped thatched roof and there are carved wooden horsemen at either side to guard the deity. Such processional chariots are particularly important in the temple rituals of South India and Orissa, probably giving rise to the tribal equivalent here.

The tribal belt continues east into the hilly jungles of western Orissa, home of several important communities, some speaking Austro-Asiatic languages from a linguistic group including Vietnamese and Khmer common to eastern India and southeast Asia. Numerically most important are Kondhs and Santals. The former are Dravidians, their name deriving from the Telugu word for a hill. Their houses, often with roofs and walls of wooden planks plastered over with mud and dung, are arranged in rows, creating streets between. Each interior is divided in two, partitioned by railings. There is an *attu* (loft), also made of planks, on which goods are stored. A wooden platform supports a granary. Some Kondh groups have a separate room for menstruating women.

These houses differ from those of most other tribals in that, rectangular in plan, they have gabled or hipped roofs. There are two verandahs, of which that at the rear is used for the pigsty and goat pen. The roof planks are covered with a thick layer of mud on which locally made tiles are set whilst the surface is still wet. The red mud which plasters the outer walls is burnished with a special stone. New houses are usually built in the month of *phagun* (March) at the end of the winter, when the monsoon grass is dry and agricultural work is light. A *dishari* (astrologer) must be consulted to choose the best date for grass-thatching.

When a new village is planned, elders test prospective sites by burying rice grains in a pit overnight, then digging them up to examine the omens. If the rice grains appear to have been moved the site is not auspicious. The village cremation ground is always situated about 500 yards to the north. The Kondhs, in common with many tribal communities of eastern India, build communal dormitories for the youth of the village. From the age of eight to ten until marriage the children, divided by sex, sleep together.

Santals comprise an important tribal group in eastern Bihar, western Bengal and Orissa. Their villages tend to be large, set out in a linear pattern of streets, each house rectangular or L-shaped, designed to house cattle and goats as well as the family. The walls are built either of slabs of mud arranged in courses or of sun-dried mud brick. The exterior is colourfully painted in red and yellow ochres arranged in rectangles, stripes and triangles. The plinth, however, is characteristically grey, achieved by mixing ash from burnt bamboo and straw with the usual mud plaster. The innermost room is a store for grain bins, with one corner set aside for ancestor worship. There is a sacred area, the *jahara*, usually amongst a grove of trees, where deities are represented by stones.

Another important Orissan tribal group, linguistically Austro-Asiatic, is the Saora, divided into nine endogamous units. Villages are always built in relation to a hill – either on its slope, peak or foot – and near a stream. The settlement plan is variable: sometimes a seemingly disordered knot of houses, sometimes linear, either forming streets or several rows looking out over the view. Each house is solidly constructed of stone or rubble, and mortared and plastered with mud. Rectangular in plan, it stands on a high plinth and often has a back as well as a front door, each with a verandah. It is low, usually thatched with paddy straw.

The main room of a Saora house is largely divided by a wooden platform, creating a low loft, and cramping the space beneath where the hearth is located. Here the grain bins and various family goods are stored. Lighter possessions such as baskets, gourds, clothes or umbrellas are suspended from the rafters. Special baskets hanging against the walls contain clothes of dead ancestors or tutelaries. The Saora have a rich tradition of figurative painting, the subjects usually referring to religious rites. These pictures, painted in white on the mud plaster, are immediately reminiscent of those of the Warlis. 'Every Saora house is in a sense a temple, for nearly every sacrifice begins indoors. The ancestors use it as a hostelry on their visits to earth.' (Verrier Elwin, *Religion of an Indian Tribe*, pp. 39–40)

Amongst Orissan tribes the Bonda are the least numerous – there are only some 6000 in Koraput district – and they are deemed to be the most primitive. The name is

Certain communities decorate the outer walls of their mud houses with paintings, often executed in ochres, ash or rice paste. Such powerful floral designs, here a kadamba *tree, are common amongst Orissan tribals.*

Mud-built kachha *housing can be as solid as stone* pukka. *Thick mud walls allow for the openings to be deeply inset, for metal bars in the window and a solid carved door set in a door surround and locked by a common bolt form. The whole is raised on a plinth of mud and stone rubble. Women are generally responsible for plastering and painting the walls. Kurli, Orissa.*

given by caste Hindus, derived from a word meaning 'naked folk'. To themselves they are 'Remo'. Elwin describes the homestead:

> The Bonda house is a self-contained unit in a strongly communal and democratic setting. Nearly every house has some sort of fence around it. The walls are of mud with a number of wooden pillars supporting the roof which is thatched with grass. The verandah is fenced in with an unplastered bamboo wall.

Bonda settlements are laid out up or along a hillside, the houses close together. Sometimes the whole village is enclosed by a bamboo fence beyond which are plots where plantain, castor and vegetables are grown. The compound in front of each house is used for many domestic chores, such as husking, cleaning and grinding the rice and millet, making mats and, in the warmer, drier weather, sleeping. The interior is usually divided, with one corner of the inner room being set aside as a shrine in which the household deity is represented by a branch of *Eugenia jambolina*, a fragrant bush of the myrtle family, along with a gourd.

The Bonda have a tradition of dormitories for both sexes. That for the girls, known as *selani dingo*, used to stand outside the village but is now integrated into it. The boys' dormitory is called *ingersin*. Premarital sex is taboo but boys can visit the *selani dingo* of neighbouring settlements to socialize, play music and dance with the girls. This leads to a boy committing himself to a girl who, if she allows him to force a bangle onto her wrist, accepts him as her husband.

Another Orissan tribe, the Juang, habitually shifts its settlements in search of better agricultural land. When founding a new village the community combine to build a house for the headman and the *nigam*, the religious preceptor. They also combine to make a *mandaghar* or *majang*, the boys' dormitory. In front of this four beautifully carved wooden pillars are put up, the central two representing the guardian deities, Buram Burah and Buram Burhi. These overlook an open area which becomes the dancing ground, set aside for the youth of the village. A flat stone is placed by the *nigam* at one corner of this ground, intended to represent the mother-goddess, Gram-siri. Only after this communal focus of the village is established can the individuals embark on their own houses.

Also in Orissa, settlements of the Gadaba tribe are arranged around the headman's house, always the largest, which is also used for village meetings. They build three forms of house, one of which, known as *chhendi dien*, is circular, centring on a tall *saal* pole from which bamboo or *saal* rafters radiate. The structure is lashed together with bark from the *siali* creeper and thatched with *piri* grass. A jackwood door opens into the largest room. The exterior walls are usually colourfully painted with ochres.

Often craftsmen serving these tribals belong to a separate community, just as they form separate castes elsewhere in the country. They may belong to Hindu castes, like the potters or weavers, or they may constitute a separate tribal group, as do the Agarias, an iron-smelting community in Bastar. Each adapts his dwelling to his craft. The potters, *kumhar*, build a roofed, open-sided area where they can work safe from sun and rain, although the verandah may serve this function.

The kiln, usually a temporary affair rebuilt for each firing, is behind the house. Fragments of pot are integrated into the walls of potter houses and compounds,

Right:
A small stone-rubble cottage roofed with roughly shaped slates. Above each window a sun shade has been fashioned from the same cleaved stone set in the fabric. The platform in front of the house forms an extension to the work area, here with a spinning wheel on the left. A tree to provide shade is cherished within a low wall. Stone slabs, important in paving, walling and roofing, are stacked to the right. Chanderi, Madhya Pradesh.

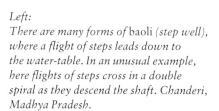

Left:
There are many forms of baoli (step well), where a flight of steps leads down to the water-table. In an unusual example, here flights of steps cross in a double spiral as they descend the shaft. Chanderi, Madhya Pradesh.

giving them a characteristic bulging appearance. Agarias use a similar open-sided structure for their forge. Weavers manufacture textiles fashioned for a particular community, such as the geometrically patterned loincloths of the Rathwa. Their pit-loom and spinning wheel are set on the verandah.

More sophisticated weavers, such as the Muslims who make the valuable silk saris of Chanderi, a small town in western Madhya Pradesh, have pit-looms inside the house, ill-lit for such fine work. The leatherworkers of Kohlapur (southwest Maharashtra), famous throughout India for their sandals, 'Kohlapuri chappals', build with sun-dried blocks made by pounding mud and pebbles into large square moulds. They work in a large room at the front of the house. The smaller kitchen and dwelling areas are relegated to the rear of the building.

Nomads pass through much of northern and central India, some itinerant craftsmen, others herdsmen moving with their flocks. Interesting amongst the latter are the Banjara, who for centuries prospered as the carriers of grain and other supplies throughout the land. The days of their bullock caravans have long gone, finally ended by the coming of rail transport, but their past prosperity is still fixed in folk memory. Handsome derelict monuments are often attributed (usually falsely) to Banjaras by local villagers. The community continues to wander as gypsies, setting village dogs howling as they pass. Their *charpoys* (bed-frames), on which perch goat kids, chickens and children, are lashed across their donkeys' backs. Goats and a couple of large dogs complete the party. Their housing consists of low tents made up of a multitude of brightly coloured pieces of cloth, in front of which they build a hearth. Banjaras, whose many different groups together form the largest nomadic community in all India, live mainly in the western Deccan. The womenfolk are particularly remarkable for their bright clothing decorated with mirrors.

Central India remains the tribal heartland, but these separate cultures are threatened by an increasing homogenization caused by rapidly improving communication and migration to cities in search of work. There, the tribals set up encampments using the most freely available materials to reproduce their familiar house forms. Many choose grinding urban poverty in preference to the struggle with some of the least productive land in the country.

In the aftermath of a destructive earthquake in the Latur region of southeast Maharashtra in 1993, attention was focused on the reasons for the high mortality rate. Stone forms an important element in the construction of both *kachha* and semi-*pukka* houses in which 88 per cent of the regional population live. The houses have thick walls, in part reflecting family status. These walls, apart from providing good insulation, increase security from burglars and also provide space where wealthy inhabitants conceal their valuables. The wall is constructed in two parts, the cavity between filled with rubble. Before the earthquake a shortage of suitable large stones meant that there were few binders to hold the inner and outer walls together. Shortage of timber resulted in fewer and more flimsy pillars than was customary, increasing the weight resting on the walls. The typical roof consists of 12 to 18 inches of earth and pebbles on a timber understructure. When the earthquake struck the supports were not stable enough to prevent hundreds of people perishing under

fallen earthen roofs and stone walls. Older houses with more timberwork than the normal load required often survived the shock.

In the more fertile alluvial lands of Central India live the Aryans' descendants, now much mixed, Hindus alongside a Muslim minority. Here towns and cities grew up, drawing in tribals as cheap labour when agricultural work was slack. Urban domestic architecture ranges from slums made up of transplanted tribal hutments to local *haveli* variants and palaces.

In the middle of the first millennium Buddhists settled in the Deccan, setting up cave monasteries, most famously at Ajanta (Maharashtra) and Bagh (Madhya Pradesh). As elsewhere, these followed contemporary wooden structures in form and decoration. They also built *stupas* (reliquary mounds) gradually encased in increasingly ornate masonry, as at Sanchi (Madhya Pradesh). The Hindus and Jains, too, carved the grey lava into caves, and even into whole free-standing temples, as at Ellora (Maharashtra). Sculptural and painted decoration at these sites give a glimpse into the house forms of the middle of the first millennium, showing town houses and thatched huts.

Islamic influence stretches back many years in Central India. During the fourteenth century Muslim governors founded states in Karnataka and Maharashtra (the Bahmani kingdoms) and Malwa, in Madhya Pradesh. One large Muslim kingdom, Bhopal, survived here until Independence.

Central India became the area of most persistent unrest for the Mughals. The emperor Aurangzeb, with his uncompromising Islamic rule, set the seal on the regime's fate. In Maharashtra a new Hindu leader rose from humble stock. Shivaji (1627–80) led his Maratha people in a series of revolts against Aurangzeb's rule. The Marathas, under a series of Brahmin *Peshwas* or prime ministers, extended their influence through much of India from Thanjavur (Tamil Nadu) in the south to beyond Delhi in the north. Divisions gave rise to four great clans – Gaekwads of Baroda (Gujarat), Scindhias of Gwalior and Holkars of Indore (both in Madhya Pradesh) and Bhonslas of Nagpur (Maharashtra). Orissa, retaining a quite separate culture and script and bounded by its thickly wooded hills, was partially protected from events in the rest of northern and central India. Here an individual form of temple architecture developed and pre-Mughal artistic forms were cherished.

Pukka domestic buildings vary considerably over such a wide stretch of country. In the west, near the forested Ghats, timber-framed brick mansions house the wealthy merchants, with fine existing examples in Ujjain (Madhya Pradesh), Nasik and Pune (Maharashtra). In Ujjain very handsome wood-framed houses survive in Bohrawad – the *wada* or quarter of the Bohra Muslims. The Bohras are a sect of Islam quite distinctive in their customs and dress, following a liberal path. The men wear little round pillbox-like hats, often white with golden decoration, and they are usually involved with business. Their quarter in Ujjain is a classical ghetto, entered by several small doorways passing through houses, and centred on a smart new mosque. The older Bohra houses resemble those in Gujarat, with heavily carved woodwork on the visible exterior and windows opening through wooden cusped arches. Later, they built larger mansions liberally stuccoed, often with Western motifs.

Brickwork is often used effectively to break the monotony of a large expanse of wall. Here, at intervals courses have been laid vertically and a feature created on the gable end by two courses of projecting bricks enclosing a course set diagonally with their corners projecting. Relief arcs above the main windows break the straight lines. Nasik. Maharashtra.

Nasik, some 20 miles from the source of the River Godavari, is a holy place for Hindus, consequently having a large population of Brahmins, some wealthy, and a prosperous business community. In the narrow climbing backstreets near Panchawati, the holy bathing place where the river passes through the town, some beautiful, if often dilapidated, timber-framed houses remain. Each encloses a true courtyard, the focus of the house, although, due to shortage of space in this long-crowded town, this is small. The verandah is sheltered by a projecting upper storey supported by carved timber pillars. There may be an *otla* (sitting platform) in front of the house, a semi-private area where the occupants socialize with their neighbours in the evening. Access to the upper floors is by an open flight of wooden steps at one side of the courtyard. Guests are entertained and business carried out in a room in the front of the house, immediately inside the door.

Pune (Poona in British days) was the Maratha capital and as such an important city in the late eighteenth and early nineteenth centuries. Divided into nineteen *peths* or quarters, some named after days of the week, it contains the brick *wadas* (mansions) of wealthy landowners or merchants. Perched on a high stone plinth a *wada* is laid out much like the North Indian *haveli*, with two courtyards, innermost being the private *zenana* (women's area). External ornament is limited to finely carved woodwork, making features of the front door, with the brackets supporting a projecting upper floor and the window frames on the upper floor. Carved in the centre of the lintel of a Hindu house is a deity, generally Ganesh, or a *purnakalasha*, an overflowing pot representing Lakshmi, goddess of fortune, an ancient motif common in temple decoration.

On either side of the entrance passage to a *wada* there are *dewadis* or guardrooms for controlling access. The first courtyard often had a fountain at its centre, functioning by gravity. Water, sometimes piped from a considerable distance, was raised to a roof-top tank by a 'Persian wheel'. Still occasionally used for irrigation this consists of a rope-tied loop of earthen pots hanging into a well. Bullocks turn a horizontal wheel which is cogged to a vertical one holding the loop. This rotates, filling the pots at the bottom, bearing them up and spilling their contents into a channel before descending again.

The court is surrounded by open-fronted rooms beyond which are office, stores and rooms for guests. The *madhyagriha* – private inner court – usually has a well. The rooms surrounding it are involved with women's daily tasks: a kitchen and stores for grain, utensils, fuel and so on.

In large *wadas* there are two further floors, reached by a narrow staircase. On the first is a *diwankhana*, the house's showpiece, used for formal entertainment and celebration of religious rituals. A rectangular hall with ornate pillars supporting arches, it is well lit by arched windows. Here decoration reaches its height with chandeliers and glass paintings to grace the walls and even including a fountain set in a patterned stone floor. The *diwankhana* of Rastewada, one of the grandest of all Pune's mansions, is actually a separate building. Although there may be a place from which the womenfolk can view proceedings this is essentially a male, semi-public room. The women have a similar, but smaller and less ornate *diwankhana* sometimes decorated with religious murals. Traditional *wadas* continued to be built

The god, Ganesh, Lord of Beginnings, is invoked first in all Hindu rituals. Similarly, he presides over the entrance of most Hindu houses, set in or above the lintel.

Above right:
'Roman' tiles used two ways: on a simple two-slope roof and on a four-slope roof divided into two sections. The upper section of the latter usually rises above the central chamber of the house, the gap between the two allowing for ventilation. A shrine stands in the street. Palaspani, Madhya Pradesh.

Below right:
The door leads through into a compound where firewood is stored and animals are kept at night. The enclosing fence is made of neatly interwoven bamboo splits. A break in the tiles prevents having to stoop under the low eaves. The ridge tiles are cemented to prevent leakage. Palaspani, Madhya Pradesh.

until shortly before Independence and are still cherished by families who can afford their upkeep but, as elsewhere in India, a transformation in lifestyle during the past fifty years has made them redundant. The joint family system has often been replaced by a nuclear family, as they move to distant towns or cities for suitable work. The large area taken up by a *wada* is a luxury in a prosperous city such as Pune. Some are rented out. Phadkewada, built by one of the Peshwa's generals, is now divided amongst seventeen tenant families. Purandarewada is owned by several brothers, all living elsewhere. Each owns a section and all are locked. Most *wadas* have suffered from insensitive alteration to adapt them to modern conditions. Amongst the few which have escaped is Naikwada, built in the 1830s by a family from Rajasthan. Here, the *diwankhana* is a large hall richly supplied with Victorian furniture, alien but fashionable during the nineteenth century.

Away from the coastal *ghats*, timber – although once plentiful, not of high quality – plays a smaller architectural role. At Maheshwar, a small holy place on the Narmada River, the two-storey houses are of locally baked brick arranged in places to provide ventilating *jalis*. Set in the side walls, timber beams mark the first floor,

The tiled roof has been broken here to allow easier access without ducking under the eave. To retain a sheltered porch, the gap has been covered by a pitched 'roof' made of large leaves held in place by poles overlying them. The interior of the house is solid-walled but the extensive enclosed verandah has an open wattle wall, providing illumination. Palaspani, Madhya Pradesh.

Above left:
A balcony and its supporting strut are both
sustained by timbers set into the brickwork
quite independently of the upper-floor joists.
Maheshwar, Madhya Pradesh.

Above right:
Struts are rarely left plain, although the
carving often reduces their strength as
supports. Both peacock and parrot are
auspicious, the latter being a messenger of
love. Maheshwar, Madhya Pradesh.

their rectangular ends forming a feature along the facade. The rectangular openings are wood-framed. Wooden struts, often fashioned as parrots, their bases resting on timbers set deep in the brickwork, support the eaves of a gently pitched roof covered with *deshi* (locally made) tiles, either flat and lipped, rounded wheel-thrown, or a combination of both. They rest on brushwood on bamboo laths bound to the rafters with twine. The windows, unglazed, are closed by solid wooden shutters, often above a panel carved with some decorative motif. Some of these houses have a balcony in front of the upper rooms, the roof extending over it on wooden pillars. A second, single-storey block behind the house is used in part for livestock. Walls connecting the two buildings conceal a courtyard.

These functional houses contrast with the Rajawada, a minor royal residence, built by Ahiliya Bai, Rani of Indore (died 1795). Here the use of timber, including imported teak, is abundant. On the ground floor, around the courtyard, wooden pillars, set in stone bases, support massive primary and secondary beams. Above these are joists and a ceiling of planks on which rests a thick layer of mud and rubble forming the floor of the upper rooms. These are reached by a flight of steps running up either side of the main entrance.

The capital of Madhya Pradesh, Bhopal, was a Muslim city ruled by an Afghan in the service of the emperor Aurangzeb. As disorder followed the death of emperor Bahadur Shah in 1712 he established himself as independent *nawab* of a separate state.

The older houses of the city are built with a projecting upper facade sustained on extended beams. The lower walls are of roughly shaped stone set in lime mortar whilst the higher sections are of brick although sometimes brick and stone alternate. For increased stability the bricks are made in different sizes. Those used low in the structure are larger and thinner, say 10 by 5½ by 1½ inches, whilst those higher up the wall are smaller and thicker, 9 by 5½ by 2½ inches. The bricks radiate to form arches, sometimes with a 'keystone' of horizontal bricks at the apex. The brickwork

Left:
The fifteenth-century palace Man Mandir integrated Muslim vocabulary into a Hindu structure. Arches, domes and tiles are mixed with trabeate, having an influence on local architecture. Gwalior, Madhya Pradesh.

Above:
The Gohar Mahal, a glorified haveli. *The whole building is inward-looking, with rooms giving onto a series of large courtyards which lead to the principal apartments beneath the high pent roof. Bhopal, Madhya Pradesh.*

is often decoratively laid to make ventilators or *jalis*. Thin traditional bricks may be set diagonally in alternate directions creating triangular apertures with a course of horizontal bricks between each course of triangles. In alternate courses bricks are set on their sides, with their axes at right angles to the line of the wall, to make small, square openings. On either side of the second-floor openings onto the balcony there are little ogee or cusped arch recesses intended to hold lamps. The pitched roof is covered with locally thrown tiles.

Most older *havelis* have perished but the remnants of Syed Shah Hussein's *haveli*, some two hundred years old, still stands in Gujarpura. Its great gateway, built of stone ashlar and brick, bears traces of ochre paintings, including a large auspicious fish on either side of the archway. It opens onto the road at right angles to the facade of the house, further protecting the privacy of the inner court. The gateways of some Bhopal *havelis* have a little two-leafed round-topped wicket set at the junction of the doors so that one small leaf hinges in each great leaf. The finest old *haveli* in Bhopal is Gohar Mahal, built beside the artificial lake. Each corner of the two-storeyed building is encased in an octagonal turret. The door opens into a flat-ceilinged porch beyond which is a forecourt with a *jharokha* giving onto its right side. This court functioned as the hall of audience. The *dalan* on the west side of the forecourt opens onto it through seven arches instead of the usual three. Beyond it is the inner courtyard with an octagonal red sandstone fountain at its centre. This is overlooked by a *baithak* (sitting room) on the second floor. Here the ceiling is partly made up of planks, partly of flat stones shaped to bridge the one-foot gap between joists, together supporting the masonry above.

Hindu domestic architecture reached its peak with Rajput palaces at Gwalior, Orchha and Datia (all in Madhya Pradesh). Built between the fifteenth and early seventeenth centuries they incorporate a division of sexes which may predate the *purdah* of Islam. There is evidence, however, that each *zenana* (women's quarters) was adapted and *jali* windows added. The *mardana* (men's quarters) comprises a *diwan-i-khas* and a *diwan-i-aam*, halls of private and public audience respectively. Amongst the private apartments there is usually a *chitrashala* (a painted room) and a private temple. Adjoining the palace stand stables, barracks, a *topkhana* (cannon store) and *daulatkhana* (treasury).

Central India's traditional buildings, as those elsewhere in the country, are under threat. In the 1920s and 1930s local builders adapted newly available materials to still-traditional forms. These included glass, often coloured or frosted, and mass-produced coloured tile. Upper-storey facades often juxtaposed brightly painted woodwork with large expanses of glass. But soon these buildings were outmoded by cement, which virtually swept away the old forms. Those that remain are further threatened by a growing demand for carved woodwork in the antique market. Much is sold to the urban rich, much is exported. Dealers offer high prices for old woodwork and some of the best collections of urban housing suffer in consequence. Many inhabitants of Ujjain's Bohrawad have happily sold the old beams and door surrounds from their houses to help finance newer, smarter, homes, made from concrete reinforced with steel.

CHAPTER SEVEN

THE DRAVIDIAN SOUTH

*Andhra Pradesh,
Karnataka, Goa,
Kerala, Tamil Nadu
and the Islands*

SOUTH INDIA is divided into five states: Andhra Pradesh, Tamil Nadu, Karnataka, Kerala and Goa. Two archipelagos lie off the peninsula: the Andaman and Nicobar Islands to the east and the Lakshadweep group to the west. Dravidians, descendants of a pre-Aryan wave of invaders, dominate the mainland. They drove earlier inhabitants before them, then were either absorbed by the Aryan influx, or driven further southwards.

Dravidian languages, although rich in Sanskrit words, are unlike those of the centre and north, but the scripts derive from a common root. Although Hinduism grew to be pre-eminent in the South and Sanskrit scriptures were adopted, there were differences in interpretation. Architecturally, too, the the region differs, its culture preserved from the violent clash with Islam which so transformed North India.

Not that the South was free from outside influences; they were plentiful. The Malabar coast of modern Kerala, in particular, became a busy centre of international trade. The Romans traded here. So did the Chinese before they confined themselves within their own seas. Arab and European traders brought new faiths so that ancient Jewish, Christian and Muslim communities flourished peacefully and harmoniously. Despite differences of religion, both settlers and converts remained largely in the cultural mainstream. Mosques and churches followed a rich vernacular style. Later, powerful external forces influenced religious architecture. Foremost were Christians from Portugal, other European colonists, and Muslims from the expanding Mughal Empire.

Prior to the British, no northern imperial power had succeeded in bringing the tip of the peninsula under a united Indian regime. During the late seventeenth century the Mughal emperor Aurangzeb became bogged down fighting the Marathas in Central India. His army failed to advance further. British rule brought the South into the mainstream, and exposed it to innovative colonial architecture.

Southern *kachha* buildings vary considerably. Along the coastal plain of Andhra Pradesh some are circular in plan with high thatched conical roofs. Others in the same village may be rectangular with two- or four-pitch roofs. Built of mud or mud and wattle, the house is raised on a plinth decorated with finger marks in white rice paste or vertical stripes of white and red ochre. Such stripes are a feature of southern buildings and are painted on temple as well as compound walls. Especially at times of festival women draw white *kollam* (auspicious patterns) on the ground outside the door. Thickly thatched, the roof projects and, particularly in the northeast of the state, comes down very low on all sides, even at the entrance. The shortest adult must stoop sharply before entering – seemingly impractical, this arrangement makes the house more weather-tight in an area prone to cyclones and heavy rainfall.

Following pages:
Settlements in coastal Kerala are spread out through the groves of coconut palms so vital in the local economy. Walls and fences are made from woven coconut palm leaves. It is a land of waterways. Pukka houses are built of laterite, with a steeply pent roof reaching out well over the walls, throwing the torrential monsoon rain clear of the house. The new building uses breeze blocks.

137

The interior is divided into two or three rooms. Alongside houses are basketwork thatched stores for fodder or fuel and open-sided rectangular or round cattle-sheds, some recently adapted into chicken batteries. More substantial houses are roofed with factory-made tiles, but some still have the local variety, small and moulded. These often combine two types, V-shaped for the lower rows running down the slope, rounded for the upper.

Thatch in Tamil Nadu is secured with twine made of paddy straw or coir which is tied diagonally over the roof. In urban areas there is a modern touch in the use of old cycle tyres lashed over the ridge to hold down the thatch. Rectangular house form varies little from that of Andhra Pradesh except that the eaves accommodate the entrance, either curving up above it or projecting in a pointed gable porch. Local tiles are commonly used but often without specific ridge tiles. Instead, normal tiles are arranged, overlapping, along the ridge. The result is inefficient. The ridge tiles tend to leak and many householders set them in cement.

The poorer *kaccha* housing uses cheap timber, palm, paddy or grass thatch and mud. Along the coast, where coconut palms are plentiful, woven panels of the leaves are used extensively as a major roofing and walling material. They are fixed, tile-like, at six-inch intervals on the bamboo roof frame, and at more widely spaced intervals for walls. Each small house has a verandah or a sheltered porch. In higher parts of the state, where palms and paddy are absent, grass provides thatching material. Often settlements are built beside the road on ground that falls away sharply. A level floor is achieved by raising the rear of the house on bamboo stilts.

Many people who work on Kerala's extensive backwaters, transporting goods or passengers, live in a traditional houseboat. Resembling a long, black canoe, this has a handsome shaped bow and stern. Most of the body is covered by a high rounded roof of woven coconut fronds. A panel at the centre of either side hinges upwards as a door shutter. Recently such boats have been adapted for tourists for quiet cruises through the backwaters.

'Chinese' fishing nets, found throughout the backwaters of Kerala, and most famously at Cochin, take their name from Chinese traders who are presumed to have introduced them along with new building forms several hundred years ago. The nets are suspended from two outstretched booms pivoted into the water from the shore, and drawn up again with the aid of counterweights.

The coastal fishing communities build similarly all round the peninsula, each settlement being in easy contact with its neighbours. Houses are made with walls of woven coconut-frond panels, or loosely packed palmyra or coconut leaves. These are bound with coir twine onto a wooden frame, the ridge pole supported by naturally forked uprights. The roof is of palm leaf, or paddy thatch over a palm leaf base. Woven coconut leaf panels are used for fencing compounds and for doors. Bamboo splits are woven into partitions for the interior of the house as well as storage baskets. Some household tasks take place within the compound and some are communal: women sit together on common ground, for instance, and men repair boats and nets on the beach alongside their neighbours. Open-sided boat shelters and frames for drying fish to feed the community during the rough monsoon period are shoreside features of most fishing villages.

The interior of a mud-walled cottage near Madras, with auspicious designs painted on the wall. The habit persists of storing certain non-perishable food items by hanging them from beams or purlins, out of reach of rodents. In a damp climate everyday clothes are usually hung rather than stored in chests. The swinging cradle is common to many Indian communities.

Above:
The arsh *(house) of a now tiny Toda community living high in the Nilgiri Hills. The handwoven embroidered robe and hairstyle are typical of the Todas, as is their house form. In a cool, often damp environment the only opening is a tiny doorway; the roof slopes steeply.*

Below:
A Toda dairy adapts the arsh *for its semi-religious function. It bears sacred symbols and a depiction of the buffalo, formerly vital to Toda life. The marked ridging of thatch is typical of Toda buildings.*

While Dravidians dominate the South and dictate urban culture, tribal communities still inhabit some hills and jungles. In the Nilgiri Hills of northwest Tamil Nadu live the Toda and Kota, and other small tribal groups survive in the dense rainforest of Kerala's Western Ghats. The Toda are the most interesting, and least numerous, tribal people of Tamil Nadu. Thought to be descendants of an early wave of Dravidian people, they live in small, loose settlements called *mod*. Until recently, they supported themselves entirely on dairy products from their herds of buffalo. Now they have turned to agriculture. Their traditional mode of life required an annual migration to established hot weather hamlets to provide their buffalo with new pasture. Old customs are weakening and only two of these summer settlements are still used. A striking people, the women dress their hair in long ringlets on either side of the face and both sexes wear a white cotton robe crossed by broad red bands surrounded by dense black geometric embroidery. Today such clothes are mostly ceremonial and women use the traditional motifs commercially to decorate mats, tablecloths and tray cloths.

A *mod* consists of a handful of dwellings, dairy buildings and a shed to shelter calves. The dairy is modelled on an *arsh* (Toda house) and also serves as a priest's dwelling. Traditional temples, constructed as thatched cones, are now rare.

Left:
A coastal Christian dwelling, slightly raised on a plinth against monsoon flooding. The walls are entirely panelled with coconut frond sections, made by folding a frond and interweaving the leaflets of one side with those of the other. Light can penetrate and air circulate, but privacy is maintained.

Right:
On the buildings of the more affluent much of the woodwork is carved. Many of the beasts have a traditional symbolism.
From top to bottom:
• an elephant represents power and wisdom;
• a lion mask, often with plant forms extruding from the mouth, is an ancient Hindu motif seen in the earliest stone temples;
• a yali, a composite mythical beast;
• the bird form is usually either a peacock or the southern Indian version of the hamsa, sacred goose – but the head has come from a mythical yali.

Far right:
The famous Malabar gable, the open 'gablet' of a Kerala mansion, its woodwork heavily carved. The opening allows air to circulate in a hot tropical region; the projecting roof deflects torrential rain. The tiles are either factory-made 'Mangalori' or locally moulded imitations. Traditional roofing material used to be inflammable coconut fronds.
Pradmanapuram Palace, Kerala.

143

Timber structure inside the roof of a Keralan house. The purlins, finely carved, are visible at their lower extreme, exposed where they meet the struts. Lathes slot into the purlins, the whole supporting a tiled roof.

The *arsh* is quite unlike other tribal huts, its form oddly reminiscent of the *chaitya* arch of Mauryan times. Shaped like a half-cylinder it is constructed of wooden planks, bamboo, cane, reeds and grass. Either end is walled by planks set vertically. The entrance is through a rectangular opening some 2½ feet high by 2 feet wide in one end wall, made small to keep out the cold and damp in these high hills. On each side of the doorway is a raised platform, equivalent to a verandah or the Gujarati *otlo*, a semi-private area where people sit and talk.

At either end of an *arsh* the walls support strong poles, often eleven in number, running the length of the building. Over these the roof and walls are completed as a continuous curved structure. In place of wood, much of the frame is made up of long bunches of bamboo splits, lashed together by a spiral of cane or bamboo splits. At one-foot intervals a hoop of such bunches is lashed over the poles forming a rib cage. This is braced by a platform of planks, becoming the floor of the loft within. On this framework courses of sticks are tied horizontally forming the laths to which rows of thatch are lashed, giving the surface a ridged effect. The grass used in thatching is said to last up to twenty years without renewal whilst the building itself is often good for eighty years.

The interior, windowless and dark, consists of a single space. A raised earthen platform takes up much of one side to serve as a sitting and sleeping place. The hearth is the focus of the end furthest from the door.

Another Nilgiri tribal group, the Kota, are socially inferior but now economically superior to the Toda. They once served Todas and, as craftsmen, were the carpenters, blacksmiths, basket-makers and potters, even supplying musicians to play at Toda funerals. They live apart from the Toda in settlements of quite different houses. These are characteristically arranged in continuous rows along the contours of a hillside. Each house is built of stone rubble, its tiled roof descending at the front to cover a verandah, much like the dwellings of many other southern communities.

East of the peninsula in the Bay of Bengal are the Nicobar and Andaman Islands. They were inhabited wholly by aboriginal peoples some of whom, hostile to outsiders, were until very recently totally detached from the rest of the world. After the Mutiny of 1857, to isolate political opponents, the British set up a penal colony here and, in 1906, built the Cellular Gaol, now a museum to the Freedom Struggle. For most Indians, this is the only notable building on the islands.

The islanders developed their own house form which impressed the intrepid nineteenth-century traveller Fanny Parks. She landed here by chance en route to Calcutta in 1822 and said of the Nicobarese:

> Their huts are particularly well built. Fancy a great bee-hive beautifully and most carefully thatched, twelve feet in diameter, raised on poles about five feet from the ground; to the first storey you ascend by a removable ladder of bamboo; the floor is of bamboo, and springs under you in walking; the side opposite the entrance is smoked by a fire: a ladder leads to the attic, where another elastic floor completes the habitation. They sit or lie on the ground. Making baskets appears to be their only manufacture.

Many tribes on these islands have no permanent dwellings, however, being nomadic. On some unsheltered or important sites, circular huts up to fifteen feet high by thirty feet in diameter are beautifully constructed for communal use, their eaves almost reaching the ground. The Jarawa tribe of South Andaman build large huts for protection in the rainy season. These were originally intended to house a permanently burning hearth since the technology for making fire was not known.

Nicobarese villages are usually near the shore, since the sea is their primary source of food. Their houses are generally circular, raised five to seven feet on wooden piles. The floor is made of planks spread with mats. A ladder leads up into the house through the floor. The interior of the house is one large undivided room, save for a platform built in the roof where goods are stored. The most striking objects inside some houses are the *kareau*, up to lifesize figures often armed with spears, intended to scare off evil spirits. There are also figures of the various creatures – fish, pigs, birds – considered most important in their livelihood. Bundles of wood are stored under the house to be put into the next grave. On Car Nicobar a tradition developed for putting a model of a boat outside the house to indicate to visiting traders that the occupants dealt in coconuts.

Some tribes have public buildings. On Car Nicobar and Chowra near large villages there is an *alpanam*, a round temple-hut, alongside a meeting house, a lying-in house where women are confined to give birth, and a mortuary where the terminally ill are taken to die. Nearby is a cemetery where corpses are only temporarily buried before being disinterred when the flesh has decayed. The bones are stored in a communal ossuary. It is only after the transference of the remains to the ossuary that the property of the deceased can be divided amongst the heirs.

A government policy of encouraging Bengalis to settle the islands is fatal to native culture. Vernacular architecture, traditions and dress have been irreparably damaged by British and mainland intrusions.

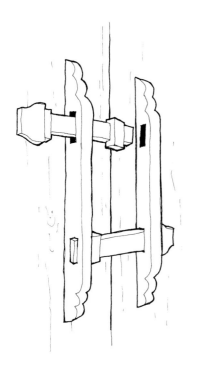

A Keralan version of the aagal, *wooden bolt, widely used to secure two-leafed doors from the inside.*

Despite ruthless overexploitation, the Western Ghats, particularly in Kerala, are a vital source of timber both for local use and for export. The southwestern hills provided much of India's teak both for house- and boat-building. As in the pre-Islamic North, timber plays a primary role in the architecture of the west coast. Kerala was created in 1956 from three kingdoms: Malabar in the north, Cochin at the centre and Travancore in the south. It is a relatively densely populated state rich in timber, and boasts the most impressive wooden architecture in the South. Its tropical temperatures are made more uncomfortable by coastal humidity. From June to September the state is cooled by torrential monsoon rains.

Although the dominant religion is Hinduism, there are large communities of Christians, said to have first arrived with St Thomas in 52 AD, and Muslims, thanks, it is said, to seventh-century missionaries sent by the Prophet Mohammed. Even a tiny, ancient Jewish community clings on, decimated by post-Independence migration to Israel. Architecturally each faith has been deeply impressed by vernacular style. Kerala churches and mosques followed the form of local timber temples until Portuguese and Mughal contacts introduced powerful alien forms. Today, cement and steel exaggerate alien and, more recently, vernacular architecture.

The most widespread building materials are laterite cut into ashlar blocks; timber, particularly teak, coconut and jackwood; and burnt brick. For temples, but rarely in domestic buildings, local grey granite is used. Most houses are roofed in tile or thatch, made from the ubiquitous coconut palm leaf, paddy straw or grass.

In Kerala the introduction of tile and brick is often attributed to the Europeans who first reached this coast at the close of the fifteenth century. In fact, the Europeans only broke an existing royal monopoly. For centuries tiled roofs were the prerogative of royalty and temples. Similarly, brick and stone were only used for royal buildings, and earlier domestic architecture was largely of mud. The first recorded inroad into this monopoly came in 1759: the East India Company was granted the Maharaja of Malabar's permission to tile its new factory in his state, the northern part of Kerala. During the 1840s, aiming to reduce urban fires, the Maharaja of Travancore, the southern part, proclaimed that all castes could replace thatch with tile. Soon afterwards British-inspired tile factories were set up in India. Mangalore, on the southern Karnataka coast, had vast resources of suitable clay. It soon became a major centre. Moulded factory tiles, still widely known as 'Mangalori', are far stronger than their handmade village rivals. Being lighter, they require a less massive roof structure.

A striking feature of Keralan settlements is that, apart from a central bazaar and business area, the buildings are widely dispersed. Each house has a small productive compound, planted with palms, fruit trees and spices. The rich take this further, constructing a worship place, a cow shed, a separate house for guests, a granary and, in some cases, even a private water tank and cremation ground.

Keralan roofs, sometimes pitched at a steep 45 degrees, with a curved ridge from which rafters radiate at either end and gables projecting over a hipped section, suggest Chinese forms. There were ancient trading contacts between the cultures but perhaps the Keralans arrived independently at parallel solutions. In style and technique there are also remarkable similarities with Nepali timberwork.

In several parts of India, including Kerala, traditional architectural forms have been integrated into smart modern buildings. Some local features are retained in this Christian Syrian compound – the high plinth, wide covered verandah and the open Malabar gable. The large expanse of glazed window is alien. Near Kovallam, Kerala.

The basic house module is *nalukettu* (*nalu* – four; *kettu* – wings), four blocks built around a courtyard into which the roof slopes on four sides, protecting a verandah from rain and sun. This roof is supported at each corner by a pillar. The external slope descends low over the outer walls, covering another verandah at the front of the building.

Local domestic architecture is based on several treatises, particularly the fifteenth-century *Manushyalaya Chandrika*. *Tarawads*, ancestral houses of the Nair community, approximately follow their dictates. One treatise, the *Tachhushastram*,

decrees that a man wanting to build a *tarawad* should first choose another of equal or superior caste to be his master. This master helps to select a plot and perform initiation rituals. To be favourable the plot must be flat with any nearby water flowing clockwise in relation to it. It is inauspicious if circular, halfmoon-shaped or three-, five- or six-sided.

The master then picks the craftsmen. The team is led by a *sthapati* who knows the architectural rules. He decides the location of the building within the plot and lays the foundation stone. Beneath him is a *sutragrahi* (man with a measuring thread). Usually the *sthapati*'s son, he helps to interpret his ideas. There must also be a *takshaka* whose task is to reduce the wood or stone to suitable sizes. The actual construction work is left to a *vardaki*, who assembles the pieces of material into a whole.

The *tarawad* must face east and on either side of the door a demon or dragon is carved to deter evil spirits. The scriptures direct that rooms function according to their position. The *vadakkina*, a room on the north side of the courtyard, is set aside for cooking, whilst the *tekkina*, on the south side, is used for ordinary household work.

While the Nairs are cavalier in their obedience to the rules, the orthodox and ritual-conscious Nambuthiri Brahmins follow scriptural injunctions strictly when building their *illam* (homestead). The Nairs are Kerala's most important Hindu community, early Dravidian settlers originally devoted to a serpent Naga cult. Characteristically, behind each Nair *tarawad* is a small serpent shrine, *sarpu kavu*, surrounded by trees and undergrowth – a serpent grove – relics of these snake-worshipping antecedents.

Nairs, in common with several Keralan communities, have a matrilinear form of descent. They also maintain a very unusual common law marriage tradition with

Nambuthiri Brahmins, apex of the local caste system. Only the eldest son of Nambuthiri parents can marry a Brahmin girl. The rest cohabit with Nair women, their children having no rights of inheritance. Nambuthiri girls are in a worse position: they cannot marry beneath them, even with Brahmins from other states, so most are doomed to spinsterhood. Within a *tarawad* lives an extended family under a *karanavar*, the oldest male. Nair children belong to the *tarawad* of the mother, not the father.

The four blocks enclosing the *nadumuttam* (central courtyard) are each oriented towards a cardinal direction. A house is extended to accommodate a family expanding through regular and irregular alliances by adding more such modules. The main entrance should be on the east side. Scriptures advise which rooms should be in which wing; but in general Muslim, Christian and Jewish houses follow a similar plan.

The *Shastras*, ancient sacred Hindu texts, stand more as a philosophical justification for already tried architectural forms than as an attempt to enforce them. When ruling that a kitchen should be in the northeast corner of the house they recognize a basic fire precaution in a land where wood, thatch and a southwest wind prevail. A building site is governed by many scriptural regulations. An auspicious plot is square. Certain trees are favourable – but only if situated correctly from the centre of the house.

The heart of every building, according to the scriptures, is the *brahmasthalam*. This is the site of the sanctuary at the centre of a southern temple. In houses it must be left open and should coincide with the courtyard. Each building plot contains a divine spirit, the *vaastupurushan*, to be visualized as a man crouching within the site, head to northeast, feet to southwest (see p. 14). Construction must start at the foot end, the southwest corner of the house. Eight types of dwelling are listed, each suitable for a certain caste, and it is considered dangerous for those who aspire beyond their station to occupy a house inappropriate to their caste.

Mappilah Muslims, a long-established community descended from high caste converts, form an important social element in northern Kerala. Many flourished in trade. During the 1920s tensions led them to a violent confrontation with the Nairs. Mappilahs, as native Keralans, have kept to a basic vernacular style. The poorer folk live in houses of bamboo, mud and palm leaf, much like those of their Hindu neighbours. The better-off adapted the house form to their slightly different needs. Older Mappilah houses in towns such as Kozhikode (Calicut) retain a central courtyard. Later ones dispense with it, are often two-storeyed and enclose some verandah space at the front of the house. A verandah remains, but it is small in proportion to the house.

The main entrance of a traditional Mappilah house leads into a lobby, an enclosed verandah. A pair of windows, opening through three arches, gives onto the true verandah. Each of these windows has a solid wooden frame and can be closed on the inside by two heavy shutters, one folding up, the other down. The lower shutter becomes a window-seat, with a pair of legs, hinged in wood, swinging out to support it as it is lowered. The upper shutter is held by wooden catches. Some older houses have barred windows, closed internally by sliding panels. In an affluent house

this lobby section has fine woodwork, a coffered ceiling and *jali* screens giving onto the room behind.

The floor, raised above verandah level, is either paved with stone tile or coloured lime plaster. Here stands a *kinathara*, a platform some two feet above general floor level. This is a combined prayer area and sitting place. The rooms become plainer and more functional as one passes towards the women's area at the back, the most private part of the house. From one side of the semi-private lobby stairs ascend to the finest room in the house, known as *mullapuram* or *padapuram*. Used for formal entertainments, the *mullapuram* of a wealthy family is a long, finely furnished hall on the upper facade. Boasting Belgian glass chandeliers and lamps, during the day it is softly illuminated through coloured glass windows. A lower, unglazed section of the window is often a *jali* of little lathe-turned balusters.

The stairs begin as a flight of three or four masonry steps, as protection from termites, and continue with wooden treads and risers between solid side planks. They are held together by mortice-and-tenon joints, the mortice of every fourth or fifth tread passing out through the side planks to be secured by a wooden peg. There is a low handrail at either side. The stairway ascends through an opening surrounded by a low balustrade in the floor. This can be closed by a trap door.

150

Left:
Traditional Mappilah wooden mosques follow the architectural form of vernacular Hindu temples, with the axis of the building running at right angles to the qibla (Mecca-facing wall). The upper rooms are beautifully ventilated and subtly lit by 'walls' made of struts with a latticework of interlinking laths. In this hot and humid climate there are many doors along the sides, as much to create a through draught as for access. Modern additions (on the right) detract from the facade. Muchchandipalli, Kozhikode.

Below left:
Padmanabhapura Palace, Tamil Nadu. Traditional southern Indian architecture taken to its logical extreme, such as the royal palace, shows a collection of modules, each centred on its courtyard. A porch sheltered by a room sustained by pillars leads into the courtyard of the first of these modules.

Below right:
Along the tropical west coast of India lathe-turned wooden balustrades function as jali screens. An airy upper room overlooks the street.

Smaller houses often lack a courtyard but have two tiers of hipped roofing. The upper section, covering the core, is steeply sloped with a gablet at each end partially closed by fretwork panelling. This decorative *jali* sometimes bears a motif indicating the faith of the occupants – a star and crescent for Muslims, the goddess Lakshmi for Hindus. It slopes outward up to the ridge, which is often gently curved, rising at either end. This gives the house an eared appearance, accentuated by wooden or terracotta finials. These little ventilating gables disappear as one ascends the Ghats to cooler, wetter altitudes.

The roof, now generally of Mangalore tile (traditional paddy or palm leaf thatch is rare), encloses a large, insulating air space, its steep slope deflecting both overhead sun and torrential rain. The curved ridge beam, often a coconut palm trunk, encourages hot air to flow out through the gablet *jalis*. The lower level of the roof is less steeply pitched, intended to cover either a verandah or secondary rooms. If there are two storeys the roof levels are separated by an expanse of wall penetrated by wooden-shuttered, unglazed windows or a rank of struts connected by spaced slats. Both capitalize on every breath of wind in a hot, humid climate. An open dormer, acting as a chimney, often projects above the hearth.

Near the kitchen, just outside or even half in the room, is a well allowing water to be drawn without going outside. The water table is shallow and the upper shaft is lined with laterite ashlar. In the hot, humid climate people bathe frequently, so a well must also be close to the bathroom. As elsewhere in India lavatories are serviced by 'sweepers' from the bottom of the caste hierarchy. In a state with high standards of education and social awareness, these folk are moving to better things and flush systems are increasingly common. In northern Kerala, walls are built of laterite blocks but in the south wooden panelling is used. Syrian Christian houses near Kottayam, usually lacking courtyards, are notable for intricately carved facades.

Kerala's domestic architecture reaches its peak in palaces at Padmanabhapura, Mattancherry and Kayakulam. Padmanabhapura was joint capital of Travancore until 1811 when its rival, Trivandrum, usurped the role. Now in Kanya Kumari district of Tamil Nadu, Padmanabhapura (the Abode of Vishnu) owes much to Maharaja Martanda Varma who, in the mid-eighteenth century, gave the place its name. During the nineteenth century, largely neglected, the palace became dilapidated but in 1934 the queen, Maharani Setu Parvathi Bai, restored it. Externally fairly simple, it comprises a complex of handsome, pitched-roof, gabled buildings, whose granite plinths are combined with teak in the fabric. Marvellous carving, much relating to the *Ramayana* and the Hindu pantheon, is confined to the interior. Originally pieces of thin shell set in a wooden frame glazed the windows, forming little squares of translucent light. Later these were replaced by red mica. The *mantrasala* – hall of audience – has a heavily carved ceiling, its decoration centring on a figure of Gajalakshmi, the goddess Lakshmi lustrated by elephants. The floor's black polish was produced by a mixture consisting of coconut charcoal, lime, palm toddy, egg white and the gum of certain plants. Such burnished floors, often tinted red, can be seen in many Keralan houses, now made with coloured cement or plaster. Beyond the *mantrasala* is a dining room 78 yards long by only 6 yards wide. Other buildings include a *natakashala* (theatre), *poojamandapa* (prayer hall), a shrine to Saraswati, goddess of learning, and *uppirikka*, a storeyed building

Formal upper room in a Keralan palace. Well ventilated and gently lit by diffused daylight, the lower structure of the pent roof meets the curved struts, between which run ranks of laths, giving a venetian blind effect. Inside this screen a sitting platform surrounds the room. The rest of the roof cavity is closed by a coffered ceiling. The roof is supported by massive pillars and, in parts, by masonry walls.

Right:
Porch of a traditional Keralan temple raised on a high ashlar plinth. The Malabar gable is adapted into a decorative feature above the door, sheltering fine carving. The copper-tiled upper storey projects far out over the open-ribbed walls. The pillars in the foreground hold many little oil lamps at dusk.

Below:
Detail of a Kerala coffered ceiling. Great care is taken with decoration which will rarely be noticed: each lotus motif is slightly different.

richly decorated with murals. Many sections of wall consist of that striking combination of open struts and slats which keeps rooms both cool and gently lit. The whole complex is enclosed within a square of high granite ashlar wall over two miles in length.

The oldest temples in Kerala follow a Dravidian model: small, square in plan, and built of stone and brick. Exploiting a wealth of timber, the vernacular style evolved, its oldest extant examples dating from the thirteenth century. Designed by Nambudri Brahmins, Kerala's temples are quite unlike those elsewhere in India. They consist of a group of buildings with pitched roofs developed from the local house form. In major temples these include an *anakottil*, a rectangular hall to shelter processional elephants from sun and rain, and a *koothambalam* in which religious dramas, including performances of *kathakali* (the famous local dance form), can take place.

These buildings are set in a rectangular compound bounded by a low block, entered through high *gopura* (gateways) in the centre of each side facing the cardinal points. Apart from its massive construction a Keralan *gopura* shares little with that of other southern temples. It is roofed with one or more tiers of tiled roof, the ridge set across the entranceway, its walls plain. In southern architecture, the *gopura* grew to dominate temple complexes, overshadowing the central, more sacred structures.

The buildings within the compound rise from a stone base, but by far the greater structural part is in timber. The stonework is simply moulded and external timber elements are fairly plain, although struts may be shaped as *yalis* (griffons) whilst lotus and geometric forms may decorate the flat surfaces, often as *jalis*. Rectangular buildings in temples and palaces are characterized by an extension of the ridge so

Left:
Temple decoration in Kerala.

Below left:
A peculiar system of shaped struts and laths forms the lattice walls of Kerala's more ambitious traditional buildings, designed to permit the passage of light and air into the interior in a climate that remains humid throughout most of the year. Each strut links with a purlin.

Above right:
More massive wooden struts, often carved to represent mythical beasts, support the extended eaves of a traditional Keralan temple.

Below right:
A fierce, flaming mask watches over the entrance of a traditional Keralan temple from the peak of a porch roof, Kodungallor. Beneath hangs a bell by which the faithful announce their arrival to the deity. The neon strip is a ubiquitous 'improvement'.

that the open gables at either end of the roof extend out over the hipped roof below, exaggerating the 'Malabar gable'. In these buildings the extension often shelters some fine carved woodwork.

But it is within the temple buildings that Kerala's extraordinarily rich wood-carving tradition reveals itself fully. Coffered ceiling sections are deeply incised with high relief figures, lotuses or swirling forms. Pillars supporting them are lathe-turned to produce annular beading of contrasting sizes, often finished with coloured lacquer. Wall panels are alive with full-relief depictions of deities and episodes from mythology.

The temple's focus is a *srikovil* (sanctuary) enclosed in a low circular building with a conical roof often tiled in copper, crowned by a gilded finial. Its entrance is guarded by a large carved *dwarapala* (monstrous door guard) posed at either side.

A modern Keralan mosque beside a canal in Aleppey integrates traditional forms with imported European ones. The main roof is traditional, the towers alien. Malabar gables shelter foreign window forms.

Fine painted metal brackets secure a bolt across a double-leaf door. Cochin, Kerala.

Within this is a square stone *garbha griha* (inner sanctum). Despite scriptural injunctions that this should stand at the centre of the site it is often a little offset.

When built in stone or brick, the *srikovil*'s internal walls are usually decorated with murals in a graceful, mobile style not unlike that of the Ajanta caves. They are painted in a palette dominated by iron oxides and copper chloride. Wooden walls are notable for the glory of their carved decoration.

Around the *srikovil*, both inside and out, are paved walkways for ritual circumambulation of the shrine. In later temples the *srikovil* is integrated with the *namaskaramandapa* (hall of prostration), a rectangular hall which stands in front of it. The result is a rectangular plan with a semicircular rear wall. The *srikovil* and *namaskaramandapa* are surrounded by a *nalamabalam*, a corridor or a pillared hall. In front of its entrance rises the brass, copper or gilded *dwajastambha*, a flagstaff topped by a metal 'flag'.

Providing nightly illumination for the deity is a particular feature of southern temples. At dusk Brahmins light oil lamps along outer temple walls and on tall, many-tiered brass lampstands facing the entrances. Each lampstand rests on a large brass turtle, which according to the myths was the form Vishnu took to support the shaft with which the gods and demons churned the ocean. Temples in Kerala are usually closed to non-Hindus.

Following pages:
The most famous synagogue serving the now tiny Cochin Jewish community. The architecture combines local features – the coffered ceiling, two-level window and lathe-turned wooden columns – with rich imported decoration, notably the Belgian glass chandeliers and blue and white Dutch tiles.

Even Kerala's mosques are less easily visited than those elsewhere, but they can be worth the effort. A few striking vernacular examples remain. These include Kuttichirapalli and Muchchandipalli in Kozhikode and Odatheelpalli in Tellicherry. Raised on a high plinth, they adapt vernacular temple form to Islamic use. Unlike mosques elsewhere, but like both temples and churches, the focus of the building is

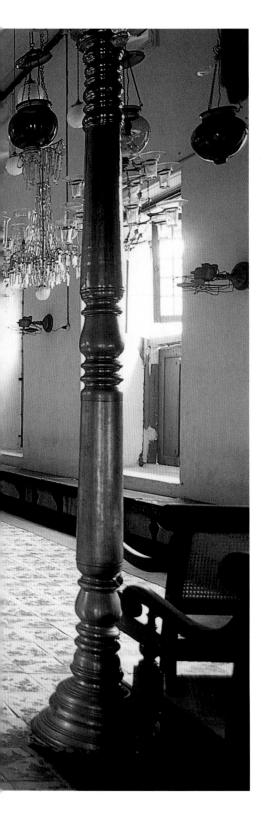

along its long axis. The *mehrab* niche where a prayer leader faces Mecca is set in a short *qibla* (Mecca-facing) wall. Vernacular mosques are unusual in lacking any form of minaret. They are airy buildings, with ground-floor walls punctuated by many openings (fourteen doorways per long side in Odatheelpalli), each with wooden shutters against the monsoon rain. The coffered ceiling, richly carved with Hindu-style plant forms, and supported by massive teak pillars, is a feature of Keralan architecture.

The mosque interior is a large open area for congregational prayer, sufficient for normal use but not for festivals such as Eid-ul-Fitr, marking the end of the Ramadan fast. An upper-floor hall accommodates the surplus congregation. Here, the roof rests on pillars as well as on a serried rank of struts curving out on all sides to support the eaves. These are set at right angles to the wall, except at the corners where they radiate. Jointed between the struts are horizontal rows of slats. At intervals this *jali* effect is broken by shuttered windows. The result is an upper floor that is beautifully cool, the light subdued. The steeply pitched roof is covered with copper tiles and its ridge bears bright brass finials.

Christianity also came early to Kerala, along with spice traders. When the Portuguese arrived here at the close of the fifteenth century they were surprised to find Christian churches already established. The vernacular form is a wooden hall, rectangular in plan, often set on a hilltop and reached by a flight of steps. But traditional wooden churches were soon abandoned in favour of Iberian-influenced cruciform-plan buildings of laterite or stone. These are the dominant older churches.

The Jewish population lives in harmony with the other faiths. The Jews of Cochin were on such good terms with the local ruler that he insisted they construct a synagogue beside his palace. One of eight local synagogues and today the focus of a tiny community, it is known as Pardesi Synagogue and dates in part from the seventeenth century. It retains such vernacular features as a hipped, tiled roof, with the upper section more steeply pitched, and a walled area between the two roof sections pierced by a number of high, shuttered windows. There is also a circular ventilator in the gable, a common feature in Cochin also seen in seventh-century temples in Karnataka. The materials are local – save for floor tiles imported from Holland. Cochin synagogues are unlike those elsewhere in having two *tebas* (pulpits), one on the upper floor in front of the women's benches and the other on the ground floor in front of the men's pews.

The 'Gutthu' houses of the land-owning Bunt community of South Canara (Karnataka) are large, inward-looking Hindu mansions. The typical house, its roof steeply pitched, combines single and double storeyed blocks around a courtyard. This is a farm house with a difference: as the isolated home of a well-to-do extended family, it is designed to deter attack. The facade is usually symmetrical around a central projection, the tallest and most impressive feature. Built principally of timber, the form persisted well into the twentieth century only to fade with the change of lifestyle.

Kodagu (Coorg) district in Karnataka is the only region of the South known for its martial people, several of whom have risen to high ranks in the Indian Army. The Kodava ancestral home, known as an *aynmane*, is impressive, standing in a surrounding compound. Always in an elevated position, it faces east. Steps lead up to a *kayyale* (verandah) where pillars supporting the tiled roof are attached to bench-like planks. The *kayyale* gives onto the *padasale*, a rectangular hall, around which the rooms are arranged. At the centre is the *mundu*, the inevitable open courtyard.

In one corner is a *kanni kombara* (prayer place), where a deity is installed. Here the *karona* (family ancestor), symbolized by a lamp, is worshipped and offered food at festivals. The kitchen is also sacred and tradition demands that the mud oven, temple-like, should face east. Benches around the courtyard, too, have a ritual significance and women are not allowed to sit on them. By the west wall of the courtyard is a niche holding a lamp and near it a hanging lamp. These stand witness to all the family events and rituals. In the morning and evening the womenfolk light and bow to them.

Near each *aynmane* is a *kaimada*, a temple-like abode of ancestors comprising a small single room entered from the east. When the *karona* is worshipped a lamp is lit, illuminating either a wooden figure or some of the man's possessions. In Keggatunadu region a raised platform for the ancestors is constructed around a tree. Several other communities build similar houses and, in common with many Hindu homes, those of higher castes – Brahmins, Vaishyas or Kodavas – have a place set aside for the sacred *tulsi* (basil) plant.

Goa became the seat of Portuguese India in 1510, and was soon dominated by large, whitewashed Iberian churches and villas. In the mid-sixteenth century the colonial rulers let the Inquisitors loose on Hindus and Muslims alike, destroying temples and mosques, forcing conversions to Christianity. Over the following centuries Portugal's imprint on local culture was strong. Laterite, palm and tile are the main traditional materials, houses often being plastered over with red lateritic clays. Some communities, such as Brahmins, incorporate a small central courtyard into their buildings, around which daily life revolves. The larger houses here, as elsewhere up the west coast, often have a verandah surrounded by an inward-looking sitting platform. The back of this seat is a balustrade of lathe-turned wooden elements, leaning outwards for comfort.

Goa's fishermen, mostly Christian, build their coastal villages in mud and palm. In a very heavy monsoon, the mud walls are threatened. They are protected by special woven palm mats, *jod mallay*, attached to the walls. Beside the house is a long, open-sided shelter for a boat. Throughout the fishing season boats line the top of the beach, but they are idle from June to September. For this period they are put away out of rain and sun.

Chettinad in southern Tamil Nadu comprises some 76 villages in a triangle bounded by Ramnad, Madurai and Pudukkottai. In an arid, unpromising landscape there are incongruous groups of huge, ornate mansions. The phenomenon parallels that of Shekhawati in Rajasthan. Here, as there, the builders are a mercantile community, many of whom have made fortunes far away from their homeland.

The merchants belonged to the Nattukkottai Chettiar community, the most successful business caste in the South. They trace their origins to the town of Kaveripumpattanam, a port in Chola times (late ninth to early eleventh centuries)

Porch of a Chettiar house. The massive, heavily carved timberwork supported by smooth, bulbous columns is a style typical of Tamil Nadu. Each pillar is set in a stone base and encircled by a brass ring to protect the wood against termites. Variable staining of the column wood enhances the contrast in form. A high platform on either side of the doorway provides a cool sitting area. Above the solid double-leafed door hangs a decorative toran.

and claim that royal persecution forced them to resettle in the environs of Madurai. Shaivites, followers of the Shiva cult, during the nineteenth and early twentieth centuries they prospered on trade with southeast Asia, especially Burma, and nearby Sri Lanka. Just as in the Shekhawati, the men settled far away to found and run businesses, leaving wives and families in the homeland. As fortunes grew they, too, repatriated profits which were spent on conspicuous building. Hence the Chettiar mansions. Today, many families, brought home by the demise of the empire which provided their immense fortunes, have settled in the larger cities of South India. They specialize in handling money as bankers and money lenders, investing some of their assets in the textile industry and in plantations. Their ties with the family homestead are stronger than those of their Rajasthani counterparts, perhaps largely due to their geographical proximity.

Most Chettinad mansions are now empty but for caretakers and the elderly, who come back to pass their last years. On ceremonial occasions, however, many family members return and, in preparation for such days, the house is revamped. One such occasion is a marriage, which is almost always celebrated in the ancestral house, at a point marked by a *kollam* (painted design) on the floor of the main courtyard.

Traditionally a Chettiar house is a large, single-storey affair, built of brick and boasting a handsome facade, in front of which, in the compound, is a well and a bathroom. The front verandah is spacious, on two levels, and covered by a tile roof

Above:
A lamp niche set into a mud wall of the facade of a village house is made a prominent feature.

Right:
Traditional festoon above a doorway. A triangular niche at either side of the door was once intended to house an oil lamp to light the entrance. The pristine state of the paintwork is a sign of the times: no one puts an oil lamp there now.

A double verandah runs along the side of an Ambular (Tamil martial caste) house. The layout varies little from a traditional Chettiar house. Bulbous pillars support upper rooms. A lighter colonnade sustains the roof draining into the courtyard. Formal meals are served here, the men sitting on the higher level. Kottaiyur, Tamil Nadu.

supported on two rows of lathe-turned wooden pillars. These are of a characteristic shape, smoothly tapering to a bulging lower section which ends abruptly in a deeply moulded neck. The wood is often stained, the smooth section light, the moulded part dark, intensifying the effect of shading. Each has a brass ring around its lowest section and is set in a stone base to discourage termites. Most of the fine timberwork is now of teak from Kerala. Whilst the Chettiars flourished in southeast Asia, the timber was almost entirely imported from Burma. Between the raised two-tier verandah steps run up to the front door. This is made a feature, panelled teak decorated with brass accessories including massive hanging ring handles. The jambs and lintels are carved in high relief with plant motifs, lions, elephants and often a frieze of *hansa* (sacred goose). This bird, the *vahanam* (vehicle) of the Creator, Brahma, is a popular subject for decorative friezes. In the South a vaguely goose-like body is given a gloriously flamboyant tail.

The Chettiar house functions around a primary rectangular courtyard, with pillared verandahs on all sides. Beside this courtyard the verandah on one side, usually that nearest to the back of the house, is used for formal meals. It is on two levels, one higher by some six inches for men, the other for women. Here guests sit on the ground with a section of banana leaf (pointed end always directed to the right) before them: on this the food is served. Etiquette requires that, when they have finished eating, they fold over the leaf towards, not away from, themselves. Behind this courtyard is another smaller one, the *kattu*, the women's domain, set aside for cooking and family meals. Off it is the kitchen, with a large stone quern nearby where boiled rice is pulped for traditional southern delicacies such as *iddli* and *dosa*. There is a well near the back of the house or integrated into it. Unlike its North Indian equivalents this house-type has a back door, set in a straight line with that at the front and those onto the courtyards. There are no intervening screens, so it is possible to see right through the house.

Small rooms are arranged along either side of the primary courtyard, each one a private room for the head of a sub-family within the joint family unit. As a mercantile community, storage of stock is important and much of the upper storey is reserved for goods. One upper room is set aside for newly-weds.

From the close of the nineteenth century until Independence the Chettiars' huge profits are reflected in the opulence of their mansions. In the later buildings there are two or more storeys, heavily embellished with stucco, carved wood or stone. Great mansions dwarf older, more elegant Chettiar houses, greedily turning to the West for decorative inspiration, sometimes cheating on the scriptures and adopting alien use of space. For example, the entrance should be on the northeast side, but this could be inconvenient where mansions face each other across a street. Often a door would be set in the northeast side merely to fulfil the law: it was not used as the entrance.

Earlier houses loosely followed the *Manaiyadi Shastras*, a Tamil text on house-building laying down the same basic cosmic rules as those applied to temples. Affluence and expansion, coupled with an awareness of other architectural forms, took a new generation of houses ever further from shastric regulations. The older homes, though smaller, boasted more courtyard space and their carved wooden beams and pillars followed traditional forms. Often the walls bore figurative murals.

Above:
Pierced stone windows, jali, *are an ancient feature of Indian architecture. A ninth-century example in a Karnataka temple incorporates the swastika and lotuses.*

Right:
Well weathered granite bulls guard a shore temple. The form of the tower – a pyramid capped with a dome – is typical of Pallava Tamil temple architecture, differing sharply from the solid sikhara *tower of north and central India. Mamallapuram.*

Left:
Across the porch of an Ambular family house. The doorway running between raised sitting platforms leads into the main courtyard. Non-vernacular features are common, such as the imported tiles. A painting of Edward VII (reigned 1901–10) probably dates the building quite accurately. Kottaiyur.

Originally floors were tiled with locally fired terracotta flags. These were replaced by real or imitation black and white marble tiles; others, bright, foreign and ceramic, decorated the walls.

The Hindu concept of a house is that of the universe as an ordered division of space ranging from vulnerable to sacred areas. There is a progression inward from the unstable to the stable, from the less pure to the pure. As a result of this the centre, the courtyard, is the most protected, sacred part. Such is the philosophy but, as with most communities, today's Chettiars have drifted from it, rarely thinking in those terms yet following the tradition to which they gave rise. Their rituals unconsciously embrace the concept. Marriages take place in the courtyard, both sacred centre and largest private space. There, too, significant contracts are agreed. The *puja* (prayer) room is nearby. Various rites enhanced the sacredness of the courtyard. It would be decorated with symbolic drawings. There was the formalized lighting of lamps and special canopies were set up for ceremonial occasions. Off the courtyard are the conjugal rooms. Until recently men and women slept separately, only using the room set apart for each head of family for intercourse.

Pollution has to be kept at bay. This involves controlling access to the sacred space. A women may not enter during her monthly periods, indeed she is usually confined outside the house in a separate small building. This system is breaking down as a result of urban living: such separation is hardly practical in a city flat. A widow, always inauspicious for Hindus, cannot attend marriages, nor is her picture permitted in the *puja* room.

The front and rear of the house are social spaces where guests can be entertained. The front, with its verandah, is the male area. Here men generally sleep, socialize and carry on their business. Women socialize on the rear verandah, close to the

A modern wrought-iron screen of Lakshmi lustrated by elephants in front of an important typical Tamil Vijayanagara-period temple. The great, towering buildings, gopura, are merely many-tiered gateways to the temple, which they have dwarfed. Madurai.

kattu (women's courtyard) where they sleep. The great Chettiar houses, during their brief reign, provided patronage for builders, carpenters, tile-makers, masons and sculptors. Now, they serve little more than a ceremonial purpose. A new generation will loosen its ties with the homeland still more. Already young men are settling further afield in search of a future. In the long term, Chettiar mansions, like those of Shekhawati, can only survive if they assume a new function.

Southern temple architecture is dominated by a Dravidian style which germinated, grew and blossomed in Tamil Nadu. Its roots were laid down in Pallava times (between the sixth and ninth century), the best early examples surviving at Mamallapuram. There, *rathas*, little shrines carved out of living rock, exhibit primary temple features – a *garbha griha* (sanctum) beneath a *vimana* (pyramidal tower) of repeated architectural forms and topped by a domed element. The finest early Dravida temple is that of Kailasanath at Kanchipuram, standing in a courtyard enclosed by high walls. In plan the temple building consists of a series of projecting and recessed bays and its walls are covered with high-relief images. These were to be characteristic features of Dravidian temples. The Chola dynasty which followed (from the ninth to the thirteenth century) developed the form further and introduced a *gopura* (gateway) which, more than any other structure, has come to typify southern temples. On a lower stone ashlar section rises a towering brick structure.

During the Vijayanagara period (mid-fourteenth to seventeenth century) its form was lost beneath tiers of brightly painted stucco figures, overshadowing the *vimana*. The quadrangle within expanded, enclosing a variety of pillared halls to house elephants, dramas, marriages and *vahanas*, wooden images of the beasts which carried particular deities. The Vijayanagara dynasty continued to enlarge temple

A southern gopura *gateway is typically a brick structure constructed on a stone ashlar basement. After completion it is covered with a multitude of stucco figures, all brightly painted. These are renewed periodically. Madurai.*

complexes. As the walled compound grew, *gopura* multiplied, being set centrally on each side of the quadrangle. Dravidian architecture reached its massive conclusion in Madurai, continuing to evolve into the seventeenth century. It was uninterrupted by waves of iconoclastic invaders which, in the twelfth century, brought northern temple development to an end.

Today, the characteristic forms are widely reproduced in shrines and temples, but the material used is generally cement. Reinforced concrete has swept middle-class South India. In Kerala it is fuelled by a flood of wealth from local migrants to highly paid jobs in the Middle East. Some houses reflect traditional forms, no longer functional, in concrete. Others only express surplus wealth. Tawdry decoration, functionless frills and alien expanses of glass appropriate to dim northern climes are the vogue. Such buildings are not only more expensive to put up, paradoxically, they require excessive energy to cool and light. Large picture windows must be veiled with thick curtains to keep out glare and heat. The true vernacular tradition here, as elsewhere, flourishes only in *kaccha* rural building.

CHAPTER EIGHT

FROM GANGA'S DELTA TO THE EASTERN HILLS

*Bengal, coastal
Orissa, Assam,
Meghalaya,
Arunachal Pradesh,
Nagaland, Manipur,
Mizoram, Tripura*

THE CLIMATE OF THE EASTERN STATES from Orissa and Bengal to the smaller ones bordering Tibet and Myanmar (Burma) ranges from humid and tropical to perennial snow. Further eastwards and higher into the hills the people become ethnically more Mongolian. To the north are the Tibetans, to the east the Burmese. Historically, these peoples were distinct from the Aryans of the Plains.

Rich deltaic soils made Bengal the richest province of the Mughal Empire. Misgovernment in late Mughal times followed by ruthless exploitation by the British during the second half of the eighteenth century destroyed the economy. Calcutta, as gateway to the populous Ganges Basin, became the focus of the British cultural invasion of North India. Bonded by a distinct culture, language and script, the Bengalis consider themselves a separate nation. In 1905 a British attempt to divide Bengal for administrative purposes had to be abandoned in the face of fierce opposition. Religion, however, became the pretext for division when India was partitioned in 1947. East Bengal, largely Muslim, threw in its lot with Pakistan, then broke away as Bangladesh. West Bengal, the populous Indian state dominated by Calcutta, capital of British India, remains economically and politically important.

Bengal's landscape is mostly flat, divided into small rectangular fields by low mud banks which retain the water essential for rice cultivation. Rich, well watered soil yields three crops a year. A typical Bengali village is a collection of hutments lost in a planted copse of fruit trees and clumps of bamboo. Vulnerable to destruction by seasonal flooding, the houses are built of light, ubiquitous materials, principally bamboo, mud and grass thatch. A rural house form, the *bangla*, influenced Mughal and Rajput architecture. Three rows of strong bamboo uprights support the central ridge and, sustaining the roof, form the basic structure of the walls. In response to a warm, humid climate, the walls are made of woven mats of split bamboo, generally covered with a mud, or mud and dung, coating. The floor inside the house is raised after the outer frame is put up, made of well rammed earth and sufficiently high to prevent flooding. Above a single, rectangular partitioned room space, a skeletal roof of bamboo beams and rafters is constructed. This roof structure is designed to curve not only along its principal longitudinal axis but also along the short and diagonal ones. The finished thatched roof has a slight longitudinal ridge but avoids ridges at the joints of each slope. The angles of the roof slope less steeply than the rest of the surface. In a wet climate, this makes them vulnerable to leaking. By lowering the corners to achieve a uniform slope local builders produced the curved ridge and eave. The eaves descend low, especially at each corner. This extended roof of thick paddy-straw thatch protects mud walls from heavy monsoon rain as well as providing shade. In some places the roof is hipped with upper gables left open for ventilation. The door frame and door itself are either of wood or bamboo.

Above left:
Village dwellings made from mud-plastered wattle walls with a two-slope paddy-thatch roof. Arable land is used for rice cultivation, but the spaces between houses are planted with fruit trees. Ponds are kept stocked with fish. Vishnupur, West Bengal.

Below left:
Aat chala *houses, with eight-sloped roofs in two tiers. The break in the roof allows for windows and ventilation of the upper floor. Vishnupur, West Bengal.*

Above right:
A fishing village, Puri, Orissa. The houses are made of bamboo and coconut fronds. Women work in a fenced compound, or communally in the 'street'. Men use the beach to make and repair boats and nets. A sail provides shade.

Below right:
A fishing village offers little resistance to high winds which constantly threaten this coast. Each house has a fenced compound. Orissa.

The roof of this basic *ek bangla* (literally one *bangla*) dwelling is copied in many larger Bengali rural houses. These are two-storeyed, a lower level of thatched roof covering a verandah surrounding the ground floor. This model is known as *aat chala* (eight slopes) and gave rise to the colonial *bangla*, the bungalow. The British needed to develop a suitable variant on their own domestic architecture to accommodate expatriates whose own tradition did not include a central courtyard. The bungalow's shaded, open verandahs followed the *aat chala* plan.

The *bangla* left its mark on the architecture of two great Indian empires. Jahangir (ruled 1605–27) introduced the form to Mughal architecture and Shah Jahan (ruled 1628–58) glorified it, reproducing it in red sandstone, white marble or whatever else was locally available. The name remains and *bangla* pavilions are seen in most later Mughal palace complexes. Rajputs, Jats and Sikhs all integrated it into their monumental vocabulary.

Bengali builders themselves adapted the familiar hut shape to create a distinctive tradition of *pukka* buildings. Under successive fifteenth- and sixteenth-century Muslim regimes the *bangla* was copied to produce a series of curved-ridge, curved-eave mosques, tombs and temples unique to Bengal. Into this basic structure they introduced an Islamic vocabulary of cusped arches, vaults and domes.

While bamboo dominated local *kachha* architecture, deforested arable land could only offer mud and clay. Brick became the main *pukka* building material. This was

Above left:
In a covered storage area a man stokes a fire sheltered by an extension of the paddy-thatch roof. Cow-dung cakes, moulded then slapped on the wall, dry for fuel. Panchmura, West Bengal.

Above right:
A narrow village gali *(alley) drains into a central gutter. The house walls are built in courses of mud and finally dung-plastered. Against a wall lean two stone discs for hand-milling grain. Vishnupur, West Bengal.*

Below left:
Auspicious hansa *(geese), a popular Hindu motif throughout India, here forming a frieze along the outer wall of a Bengali brick temple.*

Below right:
The mud-and-dung plastered walls of Orissan villages along the coastal plain are decorated with a variety of figurative and non-figurative paintings, applied by the womenfolk for certain festivals. They are painted using rice paste. Ronarak.

adapted to produce richly decorated structures. Some bricks were moulded to reproduce repetitive floral designs which frame many panels. Others were carved with reliefs of plants and figures. Along with terracotta pictorial plaques, these were fired slowly in a well ventilated kiln fuelled with tamarind wood and integrated into external walls.

Bengal is not all rich arable plain. In the southwest, the borderland abutting Bihar and Orissa is known as Chhotanagpur. Here sparsely jungled hills are still inhabited by tribal people – Santals, Bhumijs, Mandas and Oraons. Their cottages, small and thatched with wattle walls finished in a thick coat of mud and dung mix, are remarkable more for decoration than form. The walls are plastered with cow-dung and painted annually as part of autumn Diwali celebrations. As so often in India, it is women who paint, using their fingers to cover the outer walls with voluptuous imaginary flowers, animals such as peacocks and elephants, and geometric designs. These are supplemented by relief motifs worked into the mud plaster surface before it dries.

To the south of Bengal, coastal Orissa, hemmed in by jungled hills of the Eastern Ghats, was shielded from the full force of invasions crossing the northern plains. By the time invaders filtered in their impact had been softened. The poor hills support pre-Aryan tribal communities (see Chapter 6) but the coastal plain, a fertile rice-growing area, was soon absorbed by Aryan settlers. Orissa developed a distinctive temple form and cherished a style of figurative painting, seen in murals and on palm leaf, uninterrupted by Mughal or European influence.

Villages across the Orissan plain are either sheltered by a knot of productive trees rising from flat paddy fields or are hidden in extensive palm groves. The *kachha* rural house, with thick mud walls and a heavy paddy-thatch roof, is raised on a high plinth against monsoon flooding. Outer walls are heavily decorated with folk art in white rice paste. These are votive designs, painted by womenfolk for certain occasions, particularly for the harvests, in honour of Lakshmi, goddess of wealth. Some of the pictures are figurative, including depictions of the three striking Orissan idols (Krishna, his brother Balbhadra, and sister Subhadra) worshipped in the great Jagannath temple at Puri. Most, however, are mandalas and fantastic plant forms.

The Orissan temple style, reaching its peak in the eleventh century, is named after Kalinga, a regional empire, and is characterized by a *garbha griha* (sanctuary) with a massive *sikhara*. Unlike standard northern Indian towers this does not taper gradually but rises almost vertically to an abruptly rounded top. On top of this rest the crowning elements making up the *mastaka* (head), round in plan in contrast to the square tower. In front of the sanctuary is a *mandapa*, hall for worshippers, beneath a massive pyramidal roof topped by another *mastaka*. Details of Kalinga style are duly laid down in an Orissan version of *shilpa Shastra*, the scriptures relating to art and craft. In some temples, including the Surya (Sun) temple of Konarak, massive iron beams were used in construction whilst iron crampons and dowels secured stonework in place. Bhubaneswar, now state capital of Orissa, contains the finest examples of Kalinga temples.

If the Bengalis have to endure a humid climate it hardly compares with that of Meghalaya. This little hilly state points westwards like a finger, its ridge separating

Left:
A processional chariot is a traditional form of temple building reaching its apogee in South India and Orissa. A massive structure, heavily decorated with figurative carving, it is built on huge wheels. At festivals the deity is installed and menfolk earn merit by dragging it through the streets. The chariots of Jagannath temple at Puri gave rise to the English word 'juggernaut'. Puri, Orissa.

Above right:
A two-storey townhouse of about 1940. Cement replaces stucco as the decorative medium. Traditional forms remain – above each window is a chhajja (sunshade) and above that a ventilator opening and a perforated screen wall allows a draught to cool those sleeping on the roof. The ramp up the main steps is an innovation for the family cycles or motor-scooters. Bhubaneswar, Orissa.

Below right:
Bengal's brick temples turn to vernacular village architecture for basic form. Here, the aat chala (eight-slope) roof with curved eave has been copied for each element in a mandala of Shiva temples. In the background rises another basilica-like brick temple. Kalna, Bengal.

the Brahmaputra plain of Assam from Bangladesh. The Khasi Hills' southern slopes overlook flat deltaic plains so that topographically they are the first obstruction to bloated monsoon clouds as they lumber inland. Cherrapunji, a small town capping that south-facing slope, claims the highest rainfall in the world – the annual average is 457 inches and a record 905 inches fell in 1861. Although seasonal, this rainfall requires a considerable architectural response. The Khasi people, markedly more Mongolian in appearance than their Plains neighbours, established agricultural settlements in the hills. In British times Shillong, the capital, was expanded as a hill-station and missionaries converted much of the populace to Christianity.

The extreme rainfall causes Khasis to dig deep foundations for thick stone rubble house walls, protecting the interior and the wall itself from torrential flow over the ground surface. Traditionally a roof of steeply pitched paddy straw or grass thatch descended low over the walls, protecting them from the rain's full force. In such a climate thatch has to be renewed annually. Openings are reduced to a single little window-cum-ventilator and two low doors, resulting in a dark interior. Many Khasi houses are constructed of bamboo and these have a form of gambrel roof, leaving a gablet at either end. Since Independence corrugated iron, lighter and more permanent, has replaced thatch on most roofs. Tiles fashioned from flattened oil cans are also very widespread, used not only for roofing but also for wall panelling.

The Khasi community have a taboo which precludes the use of metal to join woodwork. In the absence of nails, joints are fastened either with wooden pegs or thin bamboo strips. When using wood, they prefer jackwood, wild jack and hard ironwood. A house should be built on a slope, facilitating drainage, and facing the sun. The west, place of the setting sun, has associations with death in their lore and it is very inauspicious to build facing westwards. Sites at stream or river junctions are also avoided since they are considered to be prone to visits from evil spirits.

Khasi society is largely matriarchal, women taking a prominent role in all aspects of life and inheritance passing through the female line. If a daughter builds her house in her mother's compound, as a gesture of respect it must be on the left side or behind her mother's house. A new home is inaugurated by the mother bringing a burning log to place in her daughter's hearth. To loud drumming a senior man pours a mixture of rice and rice beer over the foot of each corner post.

A traditional stone and timber house form for the wettest area is very rare since an earthquake in 1897. In plan this was square with a semicircular front. The main entrance opened through the rounded facade into a *shyngkup*, a semicircular space built at ground level. This had many general functions, including storage of utensils and an informal meeting place. Steps led from this up into the raised square section of the house. Here were two further rooms. The first, *nengpei*, combined more formal entertainment with extra sleeping space. This was the showpiece room, displaying family possessions. Beyond it, the rear space, was called a *kympei* with a hearth set centrally and beds at either side. This was the private space, closed to all but family and intimate friends. Where such houses survive thatch has given way to metal roofing. Here, this has a further disadvantage above that of heat-loss: in a region of frequent, heavy rainfall the noise can be deafening.

North of Meghalaya is the Brahmaputra plain through which, exhausted by its tumultuous descent from the Tibetan Plateau, the river wanders, breaking and rejoining, before turning sharply to join the Ganges delta. This rich, narrow plain forms the state of Assam, famous for its tea; its people are racially and linguistically distinct. It is bordered to the north by the Himalayan foothills.

The population of Assam ranges from Assamese and Bengalis to various tribal minorities. The indigenous folk feel threatened by a growing number of Bengalis, many recent migrants from Bangladesh, who differ in their culture and Muslim faith. There remains a small mercantile Marwari community from distant Rajasthan. Village homesteads are similar to those of Bengal, constructed mostly of bamboo, raised on a low plinth, with walls of mud-plastered split bamboo matting and a two-sloped pitched roof thatched with paddy straw and sheltering a front verandah.

The Bodo Kachari tribals north of Brahmaputra are fairly typical in their dwelling type. A prosperous rural homestead comprises several buildings around a small mud-smoothed compound surrounded by a high bamboo fence. This provides the private open space so cherished in the Indian domestic context. A cactus plant, *sizu*, object of devotion as home of the tribe's supreme deity, is planted on the compound's north side as the focus of family prayers. One building, the largest and dominant space, is used for sleeping and household chores. As so often in the

The suspension bridges of northeast India, communally constructed from timber, bamboo and cane rope, impressed generations of travellers. Lengths of wood keep the sides of the bridge apart and form the walkway. Bamboo splits are loosely woven into side screens and the ropes are fashioned either from crushed bamboo or cane.

Following pages
Left:
A house made almost entirely from bamboo
stands on a raised timber platform. The wall
and roof structure is of variably sized bamboo
poles, the wall panels of flattened bamboo
culms, the roof thatched with paddy straw.
Light penetrates the dim interior through the
door. A storage platform hangs beneath the
eaves. Karbi Karbi, Anglong, Assam.

Right:
The platform, of massive bamboo poles
overlain by several layers of smaller ones, is
supported by timbers and bamboo poles
which carry it out over the slope. Steps lead up
to a rear entrance sheltered by a porch.

northeast a separate building is set aside for cooking and a lean-to shed adjoining it houses a loom. Weaving is a craft that is common, although fading, amongst the tribals of the northeast and their bright, striped fabrics are a feature of the region. There is a guest house, an extra room generally used by the family but invariably given up to visitors. A granary, small and thatched, has a projecting ridge around its plinth to discourage rats.

The people of the northeastern hills are undoubtedly India's masters of bamboo architecture. As far back as the eleventh century, Chinese Buddhist pilgrims entering India by this hazardous route mention bamboo suspension bridges in their accounts. They also surprised early British travellers in the northeast. Several Nagaland and Arunachal tribes, confronted with impassable torrents, solved the problem by building such bridges. They consist of a series of oval cane hoops held between cane cables running from bank to bank. The walkway itself is made of closely woven bamboo splits, with timbers laid crossways at intervals preventing the hoops from being deformed into a V-shape under weight. At high altitudes where cane is not available, bamboo rope is used. Screens on either side of the bridge are also of bamboo, loosely woven to offer minimal resistance to the wind. In recent years the government has provided steel cables to make for safer bridges but the technique survives. As with so much building in this part of India bridge construction entails the mobilization of the whole community, each contributing according to his or her ability.

In Arunachal, houses, like those of many neighbouring hill folk, are usually built on stilts. This creates a horizontal floor surface on the hillside or ridge sites preferred for settlements. The house frame is formed of bamboo and wooden planks lashed together with bamboo splits.

The Adi Gallong folk of Siang district build facing a hilltop so that the back of the house projects over the slope. At the rear, on a raised floor platform, is a latrine. Waste falls through a hole in the floor down to pigs in a sty below who happily recycle it. This formalizes a disposal system flourishing wherever man and pig coexist. The house platform is reached by a ladder of cane rope held at a suitable stair-like angle by two leaning bamboos. The house comprises a central square room surrounded by a verandah of variable width. The room itself has no windows and is only illuminated faintly by light entering from small doors on three sides. There is a fireplace inside, consisting of earth and stones placed in a wooden box and sunk into the floor. This has a surround of dense hardwood. In this damp climate smoke from the hearth performs two functions: it cures stored meat and also protects the house fabric from rot and fungus. Timber, in a region dominated by bamboo, plays an unusually large part in local building, planks being used to reinforce the stilt foundation beneath the platform and also, lashed to bamboo supports, as walls for the central room.

Eastwards, along the border of Myanmar, in north-south sequence, are Nagaland, Manipur and Mizoram. Nagaland consists of a series of deep valleys separated by high ridges inhabited by several Naga tribes. The river gorges separate these tribes linguistically from those of the adjacent ridge. Once a small independent state, Nagaland was taken by the British and has been in sporadic insurgency

against successive Indian governments since Independence. The people, once head-hunters, now mostly Christian, have a long tradition of martial prowess.

A Naga house has an elongated rectangular plan, a short side forming the facade, either convexly curved beneath a fan of rafters or gabled and overhung by the projecting roof. The house traditionally faces in an easterly direction. Broad wooden boards forming the house front are often adorned with elaborate carving, the subjects generally drawn from wildlife, hornbills and the horns of a *mithan* (bison) being particularly popular. The head of a tusked boar, deer antlers, birds and human figures commonly feature on these boards. Each beast has a ritual or mythological significance. In Naga society men punctuate their social rites by giving feasts; the more guests, the greater the social merit. Each feasting, *genna*, entitles the giver to more ambitious adornment, not only of his person but also of his house. The right to have carved boards on the house-front is the reward for giving one such *genna*. The first performance of this ritual gives the right to having three front boards carved. If it is repeated, all can be decorated. Traditionally a human head can only be represented if the householder has taken a head in fair combat.

The type of entrance varies. A wooden or bamboo shutter is set in the doorway, opening and closing on a pivot, on hinges or by sliding. One hinge type ingeniously exploits the bamboo's natural form. The door panel sockets neatly, top and bottom, into the hollow of a fixed bamboo culm of greater diameter. Here it can rotate whilst being held firmly. Wooden door shutters are particularly richly carved.

Stairs are also made by adapting a bamboo stem, with arched holes serving as steps being cut at suitable intervals out of a massive stem. The larger part of a Naga house is floored with beaten mud. Roofs are often hog-backed, avoiding corner

Above:
Naga field rest houses. Highly decorated,
designs vary considerably from tribe to tribe.
The local bison, mithan, *is a very popular*
motif with all groups for carved woodwork.
The dramatic extended 'eave woodwork' is
typical of Chakhesang tribe buildings.

Left:
The striking curve of the eaves is typical of
certain Naga tribes.

ridges and thatched with paddy straw or, in the case of Konyak Nagas, palm leaves folded in two. Wealthier villagers prefer to tile their roofs with wooden shingles. The interior is divided by a number of woven wall panels to create rooms. A kitchen and a place for pounding and husking rice are found inside the entrance, with the sleeping rooms towards the rear.

By adding bamboo partitions the house can be adapted to cater for new requirements. Today's children, for example, need a room for school work, so a space, complete with a hitherto alien table and chair, is partitioned off. Aspirations change and success is no longer rated at the number of neighbours' heads on display.

Many bamboo-built houses in the northeast have a *machan*, an unroofed area on stilts. In Nagaland this is at the back of the house, constructed so that the *machan* projects over a slope. In dry weather it serves as extra living space as well as a drying platform. Being well lit, it is the preferred place for weaving. At one side of the platform a little 'long drop' lavatory overhangs pigs in a sty below.

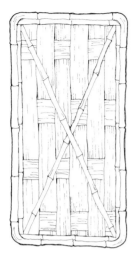

Above:
A Naga door shutter made of a bamboo frame held in place by two diagonals filled with woven, flattened bamboo.

Below:
Door opening of a Konyak tribe morung, shaped through carved wooden panelling and giving access into the unlit interior.

Unhusked grain is stored in large granaries, each belonging to an individual household. They are built singly or in clusters at the edge of a *khel* or village, some distance from the house. This is a precaution against widespread fires: lack of shelter is unpleasant, lack of food disastrous. The granary is built of wood and raised some three feet above the ground as a precaution against damp and rats. The latter are further discouraged by a circular timber plate at the top of each supporting post, acting as a staddle stone to prevent rodents climbing up. Auspicious carvings, including the ubiquitous *mithan* head, decorate the wooden facade.

Various Naga tribes create India's most spectacular bamboo architecture. The most handsome building in a Naga village is the *morung*, a communal construction confined in India to certain eastern societies. It houses unmarried youths as well as providing a hall for certain rituals. It is also the repository of tribal trophies which, until fairly recently, included human heads. This vital communal institution is fading in the face of Westernization.

Naga villages usually have a perimeter fence. Some tribes, including the Angami, have carved doors at the main village entrance. These bear carvings of men, spears, bosses representing breasts, a full moon, cows and sets of horns. In a big Naga settlement each house belongs to a *khel*, a colony made up of a knot of buildings. It is the responsibility of all the menfolk to take part in any building project within their own *khel*. They work with a *dao* (sharp-bladed knife). Bamboo is felled during the dry season (October to March) but, along with palm leaves, it is only cut under a full moon. If the *khel* has a *morung* it is always positioned higher up the hill than other buildings. A *morung* is usually large, dominating its *khel* or village, and richly ornamented with carved woodwork. In most tribes boys enter a *morung* at about six years old, staying there until marriage. It therefore houses the entire young male population, acting as guardhouse and barracks for an essentially martial people, a school for the young and a dormitory. As an institution it is alien to traditional Hindu or Muslim society but relates closely to similar establishments amongst certain Indonesian tribal communities.

A *morung* is built during the winter, everyone being mobilized whilst work is in progress, the women keeping the workers supplied with food and drink. Wood plays an important role in the structure of Naga buildings and, particularly on the *morung*, it is frequently deeply carved with powerful designs. Most popular are the horned head of a *mithan* and hornbills, which represent fertility. An upright post at the entrance of an Ao tribe *morung* usually bears a figure of a tiger, head downwards, and a *mithan* head.

Apart from the roof, which is thatched with grass or palm leaf, the rest of the building is fashioned from bamboo. A raised floor inside the *morung* is reached by steps carved in wood or cut into a large bamboo stem. Bamboo provides not only woven geometrically patterned wall panels, scaffolding, steps, partitions and neat door hinges, but also such details as pegs, roof tiles, wedges, nails and even the basic rope used to lash the whole building together. This is made from the outer layer of the fibrous stem and is used whilst fresh and damp, so that as it shrinks with drying it firmly grips the constituent parts of each joint.

There are eight major Naga tribes. The *morung* of the Angami of southwest Nagaland is a fairly simple structure of wood and thatch. That of the Ao of the north central area is no more than an ordinary house glorified with fine ornament. Those of the Chang and Konyak tribes of the northeast are the most impressive. The ridge pole is exploited to produce a curved roof-ridge rising spectacularly over the front to a sharp pointed peak supported by carved posts, a feature reminiscent of Indonesian architecture. Some *morungs* have a narrow oval opening lacking any shutter, emphasized by decoration, sometimes in colour. The thatched roof here, where rainfall can be torrential, descends low over the sides of the building. There are usually no windows, the dim interior being lit only by small door openings.

Thatch is applied as thickly as economically possible, the number of layers indicating the wealth and importance of a householder. As with all thatch, it requires renewal within the life of the house, a palm-leaf roof being reckoned to survive for some ten years. Timber uprights are arranged in rows of three, those of the centre being the tallest, projecting through and above the ridge. Their function is only to support the roof. A secondary structure of bamboo holds the wall panels.

The Thadou Kukis of Manipur, frequently in conflict with Nagas, build scattered villages in dense jungle on or just below a ridge. Before a village can be built omens and dreams are consulted. A small piece of shell is removed from one end of an egg which is placed on three sticks above a little fire. If the egg bursts the omens are bad. If it congeals on top they are good. In contrast with Naga custom there is no perimeter, wealthy villagers building their own fence to protect vegetable gardens from *mithan*. The largest house is that of the chief. This has a platform of wood and bamboo at the front on which men congregate to discuss problems and disputes.

Individual houses are built of wooden posts and rafters with a thatched grass roof held in place by bamboo splits and lashing. The back of the house stands on stilts some four to six feet up, the front resting on the ground, where a heavy mortar is used for husking rice. Field houses, which have no mortar, are raised on stilts and entered by a ladder. A mud cooking hearth some three feet square and six to nine inches deep is set in the centre of the main room, resting on the floor trusses. Cooking vessels are perched above the fire on three conical stones stood in the centre of the hearth. Above it drying platforms are hung.

CHAPTER NINE

THE FUTURE

EACH REGIME, native or foreign, which has ebbed and flowed across the subcontinent has patronized a particular architectural style. Its monuments left an impression on traditional building, especially in its *pukka* incarnation. No invader had such a cataclysmic effect as the British. They formed the vanguard of a rising Eurocentric industrialized world. British ascendancy in India was based on the revolutionary methods of industrial production being developed on their distant island. Industrialization has proved beneficial but mass-production imposes uniformity. In reaction, it brings a regret for the passing of the quirky, anachronistic individuality of home-crafted, handmade goods.

Imperial trade relied on its British industrial base fed by imported raw materials. The full impact of industrialization did not touch India until after Independence, when self-reliance became the panacea. When it came it roared through the land like a dragon. India's industrial achievements are often ignored: cement, steel girders, corrugated iron sheeting, all home-produced in bulk, were soon readily and comparatively cheaply available. Itinerant architects and powerful visual images revealed the versatility of these new materials in the dynamic, admired West. This was the modern way and, as raw materials and labour became dearer, this was also the cheap way.

Traditional mansions, no longer considered practical or comfortable in the heart of India's industrialized towns, were deserted. Their wealthy owners, in an era of improved transport, moved to concrete villas in distant suburbs. The family house was rented out. Prime urban property, it was partitioned into multitudes of tiny dwellings and offices. The palace became a slum.

The old sector of any Indian city has an air of frenetic bustle and congestion. On either side of each street buildings are lost beneath a jumble of hoardings, advertisements, film posters, notices relating to the myriad of tenants. Look more carefully. Beneath the detritus it is often possible to make out a fine facade, beautifully carved stonework, the wreckage of a once-proud *jharokha*, a handsome door-surround. Market forces have swept aside practical aesthetics.

Even when free from crowding, town houses fare little better. In Shekhawati (Rajasthan) or Chettinad (Tamil Nadu) mansions can be maintained fairly cheaply given single-ownership, personal involvement and sufficient funds. In Chettinad where most of the large mansions were built in the twentieth century, family fortunes have not radically altered and estrangement from the homeland has barely begun.

Shekhawati, its prosperity older, has travelled further down the road. Some houses have fallen into neglect, others have been sold or rented out as a number of apartments. Property division is marked by cemented walls, by concrete additions such as bathrooms and lavatories, carbuncles on a once elegant facade. In the absence of pressure from powerful, wealthy house owners, municipal administration is slack, contributing to rapid fabric decay.

Drainage was barely perceived as a problem when great *havelis* were built. In a desert, where every gallon of water had to be hauled up a deep shaft, there was little prospect of wasted water. Today, Shekhawati's towns have a pumped, piped water supply. Water flows only at certain hours of the day, so that practice is to leave one's bucket beneath an ever-open tap. The overflow runs into the street along the sides of great houses. By capillary action water passes up the masonry. Here, the salts it carries crystallize, pulverizing brick, hardpan and mortar. The main threat to Shekhawati's traditional buildings is this decay of footings. Yet, even in the small town of Mandawa, the hub of a busy tourist trade based on the painted architecture, nothing has been done to curb this destructive waste of water which is drastically lowering the water table.

Many threats to traditional buildings are, given the will, equally easily solved. Some, stemming from entrepreneurial greed, are more difficult to confront. The wealthy, both Indian and foreign, in search of a little 'ethnic' work to glorify their drawing room, have created a demand for some of the structural elements that grace older buildings. Woodwork, comparatively light and resilient, is particularly vulnerable. Carved Punjabi *jharokhas*, Shekhawati door and window surrounds, glorious Gujarati carved struts, *jali*-work from Ujjain's Bohrawad, carved pillars and ceiling panels from Kerala are all to be found in the antique market. Owners have a financial incentive to pull down old buildings, eviscerate them and build anew.

During the last two decades, as destruction has proceeded apace, there has been a growing awareness of the inherent cultural loss. Indira Gandhi took a lively interest in environmental and cultural conservation. She was partly instrumental in founding INTACH, the Indian National Trust for Art and Cultural Heritage. This organization has established chapters throughout the country and set about documenting India's wealth of traditional building. But such documentation, in the absence of any laws to back it up, merely records a fast-declining heritage. Legislation on a par with that governing graded lists of buildings in the West has to be backed by funds for grants to cover restoration in vernacular materials by local methods. It will be a long time before this comes to the fore of India's list of priorities.

Given the lack of government support, even when commercial demands such as tourism require it, conservation must turn elsewhere for action. Family pride, when coupled with wealth, can be encouraged to keep an ancestral house standing in the face of all practical considerations. Financial return is, however, the best incentive for conservation. In India the success of 'heritage hotel' projects has encouraged owners of forts and palaces to restore them to their original form and cash in on a growing tourist demand. Large merchant and *zemindar* (landowner) homes are also being adapted for tourism.

Renewed interest from architects in traditional forms and materials is a positive force towards rejecting the steel and concrete block. Old methods were thrown aside thoughtlessly, but there can be no return to the truly traditional. By its nature it was the product of local masons supplied with whatever was near the site and geared to confront the surrounding environment. It was not produced by sophisticated architects with a wide knowledge of universal solutions to structural problems.

Kaccha architecture continues to thrive. Most villagers cannot afford to leave the repertoire of mud and straw with which they have grown up. All over India mud, stone and wooden *jhonpris* (cottages) are being built in a manner varying little from those of earliest historical times. There are intrusions – 'Mangalori' tiles, standard burnt bricks, corrugated iron – but generally they do not altogether transform the structure. However, any complacency is misplaced. Where money is available people usually act on aspirations to escape what they perceive as 'rustic'. In Punjab, for instance, India's richest state, it is noticeable how little is built in mud and straw, and how many houses are rectangular blocks of standard brick. The only possible reversal for this trend is a change in the popular perception of desirable housing.

BIBLIOGRAPHY

Ali, M. H., *Observations on the Mussalmauns of India*, Oxford University Press, London 1917

Allchin, F. R. and B., *The Birth of Indian Civilisation*, Penguin Books, Harmondsworth 1968

Ananthalwar, M. A. and A. Rea, *Indian Architecture*, 3 vols, Indian Book Gallery (reprinted), Delhi 1981

Archana, *The Language of Symbols*, Crafts Council of India, Madras (n. d.)

Arshi, P. S., *Sikh Architecture in Punjab*, Intellectual Printing House, New Delhi, 1986

Bagai, R., *Towards the Sun* (unpublished thesis), D. C. Patel School of Architecture, Ahmedabad, 1988

Batley, C., *Indian Architecture*, Taraporevala (reprinted), Bombay 1994

Bernier, F., *Travels in the Mogul Empire*, Archibald Constable & Co., London 1891

Bhatia, G., *Punjabi Baroque*, Penguin Books, New Delhi 1994

Biswas, S. S., *Bishnupur*, Archaeological Survey of India, New Delhi 1992

Bourgeois, J.-L., *Spectacular Vernacular*, Aperture Foundation Inc., New York 1989

Chetwode, P., *Kulu. The End of the Inhabitable World*, John Murray, London 1972

Cooper, I. A., *The Painted Towns of Shekhawati*, Grantha Cunningham, Vol. 11, 1994

——— and B. Patadia, *Documentation of Buildings in Diu*, INTACH, New Delhi 1988 (pending publication)

——— and R. Sharma, *Documentation of Buildings in Shekhawati*, INTACH, New Delhi 1987 (pending publication)

Dani, A. H., *Thatta. Islamic Architecture*, Islamic University, Islamabad 1982

Dasgupta, P., *Temple Terracotta of Bengal*, Crafts Museum, New Delhi 1971

Dawson, B. and J. Gillow, *The Traditional Architecture of Indonesia*, Thames and Hudson, London 1994

Deloche, J., *The Ancient Bridges of India*, Sitaram Bhartia Institute of Scientific Research, New Delhi 1984

Desai, Z., *Mosques of India*, Ministry of Information and Broadcasting, New Delhi 1966

Devakunjari, D., *Hampi*, Architectural Survey of India, New Delhi 1992

Doshi, S., J. Pieper, G. Michell (eds), *The Impulse to Adorn*, Marg Publications, Bombay 1982

Drew, F., *The Jummoo and Kashmir Territories*, London 1875

Fathy, H., *Natural Energy and Vernacular Architecture*, University of Chicago Press, Chicago and London 1986

Fleming, J., H. Honour, N. Pevsner, *Penguin Dictionary of Architecture*, Penguin Books, London 1966

Grierson, G. A., *Bihar's Peasant Life*, Calcutta 1885

Guidoni, E., *Primitive Architecture*, Faber and Faber Ltd., London 1987

Haider, S., *Tilework in Pakistan*, National Institute of Folk and Traditional Heritage, Islamabad (n. d.)

Hall, N., *Thatching*, Intermediate Technology Publications, London 1988

Harcourt, A. F. P., *The Himalayan Districts of Kooloo, Lahul and Spiti*, London 1871

Harle, J. C., *The Art and Architecture of the Indian Subcontinent*, Penguin Books, Harmondsworth 1986

Howard, N. F., 'The Fortified Places of Upper Kulu, India', in *South Asian Studies* Vol. II, London 1995

Jain, A. K., *Building Systems for Low Income Housing*, Management Publishing Co., Dehra Dun 1992

Jain, K. (ed.), *Hill Settlements*, Thesis and Research Committee of School of Architecture at CEPT, Ahmedabad (n. d.)

——— and Jain, M., *Mud Architecture of the Indian Desert*, AADI Centre, Ahmedabad 1992

———, *Indian City in the Arid West*, AADI Centre, Ahmedabad 1994

Jain-Neubauer, J., *The Stepwells of Gujarat*, Abhinav Publications. New Delhi 1981

Janssen, J. J. A., *Building with Bamboo*, Intermediate Technology Publications, London 1988

Jayanetti, L., *Timber Pole Construction*, Intermediate Technology Publications, London 1990

Kak, R. C., *Ancient Monuments of Kashmir*, The India Society, London 1933

Khan, A. A., *Post-Disaster Reconstruction in Earthquake Affected Area* (unpublished), School of Architecture and Planning, New Delhi 1995

Khan, A. N., *Multan. History and Architecture*, Institute of Islamic Culture and Civilisation, Islamic University, Islamabad 1983

———, *Islamic Architecture of Pakistan*, Vol. 1, National Hijra Council, Islamabad 1990

Khushu, S., *Jhelum River Front, Srinagar* (unpublished), School of Architecture and Planning, New Delhi 1989

Kipling, J. L., 'Indian Architecture Today' in *Journal of Indian Art and Industry*, Vol. 1, Calcutta 1886

Koch, E., *Mughal Architecture*, Prestel-Verlag, Munich 1991

Koppar, D. H., *Tribal Art of the Dangs*, Department of Museums, Baroda 1971

Kramisch, S., *The Hindu Temple*, University of Calcutta, Calcutta 1946

Krishnamurthy, K., *Early Indian Secular Architecture*, New Delhi 1987

Lahiri, K., *Tripura Temples*, Saraswat Library Calcutta, 1982

Lang, A. M. (ed.), *Professional Papers of Indian Engineering*, Rurki 1872

Lari, Y., *Traditional Architecture of Thatha*, The Heritage Foundation, Karachi 1989

Lessard, G. and A. Chouinard (eds), *Bamboo Research in Asia*, International Development Research Centre, Ottawa 1980

Llewellyn-Jones, R., *A Fatal Friendship*, Oxford University Press, New Delhi 1985

Mahapatra, R. P., *Decorative Art of Parasuramesvar Temple*, Orissa State Museum, Bhubaneswar 1991

Mahapatra, S. and M. Patnaik, *Patterns of Tribal Housing*, Academy of Tribal Dialects and Culture, Bhubaneshwar 1986

Medley, J. G. (ed.), *Professional Papers of Indian Engineering*, Rurki 1864

Michell, G., *Penguin Guide to the Monuments of India*, Vol. 1, Viking, London 1989

——— (ed.), *Brick Temples of Bengal*, Princeton 1983

——— (ed.), *Masterpieces of the Deccan Sultanates*, Marg Publications, Bombay 1985

——— and S. Shah, (ed.), *Mediaeval Ahmedabad*, Marg Publications, Bombay 1988

Misra, R. L., *The Mortuary Monuments in Ancient and Medieval India*, B. R. Publishing Corp., Delhi 1991

Mitra, D., *Pandrethan, Avantipur and Martand*, Archaeological Survey of India, New Delhi 1977

Mumtaz, K. K., *Architecture in Pakistan*, Concept Media, Singapore 1985

Nair, M., *A Study of the Traditional Nair Homes of Kerala* (unpublished), D. C. Patel School of Architecture, Ahmedabad 1989

Nath, O., *Evaluation of Indira Awaas Yogana in Selected Districts of Bihar* (unpublished), School of Architecture and Planning, New Delhi 1995

Norton, J., *Building with Earth*, Intermediate Technology Publications, London 1986

Oliver, P., *Dwellings. The House Across the World*, Phaidon, Oxford 1987

Ohri, V. C., *Arts of Himachal*, State Museum, Simla 1977

Pandit, M., M. Misra, N. Raina, N. Manchanda and P. Jain, *Documentation of Vernacular Buildng Systems in the State of Jammu and Kashmir*, GRAAM, New Delhi (n. d.)

Parks, F., *Wanderings of a Pilgrim in Search of the Picturesque*, Pelham Richardson, London 1850

Patnaik, N., P. K. Mohanty and T. Sahoo, *Life in Sonabara Plateau*, Tribal and Harijan Research-cum-Training Institute, Bhubaneshwar 1984

Patnaik, N. (ed.), *The Juang*, Tribal and Harijan Research-cum-Training Institute, Bhubaneshwar 1989

——— (ed.), *The Saora*, Tribal and Harijan Research-cum-Training Institute, Bhubaneshwar 1989

Pereira, J., *Elements of Indian Architecture*, Motilal Banarsidass, New Delhi 1987

Pramar, V. S., *Haveli*, Mapin, Ahmedabad 1989

Qaisar, A. J., *Building Construction in Mughal India*, Oxford University Press, New Delhi 1988

Raina, S., *Towards Developing Guidelines for the Development of Historic Housing, Bundi* (unpublished), School of Planning and Architecture, New Delhi 1993

Ramaswami, A., *Tamil Nadu District Gazetteers. Ramnathpuram*, Madras 1972

Ramaswamy, N. I., *Understanding the Vernacular Architecture of Kerala* (unpublished), York 1992

Ranjan, M. P., N. Iyer and G. Pandya, *Bamboo and Cane*

Crafts, The Development Commissioner of Handicrafts, New Delhi 1986

Rao, S. R., *Lothal*, Archaeological Survey of India, New Delhi 1985

Rudofsky, B., *Architecture Without Architects*, Academy Editions, London 1964

Rykwert, J., *The Idea of a Town*, MIT Press, Cambridge, Massachusetts 1976

Sarma, P. C., *Architecture of Assam*, Agam Kala Prakasham, New Delhi 1989

Shwa, W., *Notes of the Thadou Kukis*, Government of Assam, Calcutta 1929

Singh, M. G., *Art and Architecture of Himachal Pradesh*, New Delhi 1983

Slesin, S. and S. Cliff, *Indian Style*, Thames and Hudson, London 1990

Soundara Rajan, K., *Temple Architecture in Kerala*, Government of Kerala, Trivandrum 1974

Tadgell, *The History of Architecture in India Architecture*, Design and Technology Press, London 1990

Tillotson, G. H. R., *The Rajput Palaces*, Yale University Press, New Haven and London 1987

————, *The Tradition of Indian Architecture*, Yale University Press, New Haven and London 1989

Tillotson, S., *Indian Mansions*, The Oleander Press, Cambridge 1994

Tikoo, A., *Traditional Timber Bridges of Srinagar*, School of Architecture and Planning, New Delhi 1987

Varuni, R., *The Community, the Settlement and the Shelter* (unpublished), D. C. Patel School of Architecture, Ahmedabad 1992

Venkata Ramanayya, N., *Origin of the South Indian Temple*, Asian Educational Services, New Delhi 1992

Varma, P. K. and S. Shankar, *Mansions at Dusk*, Spantech Publishers, New Delhi 1992

Wheeler, M., *Civilisation of the Indus Valley and Beyond*, Thames and Hudson, London 1966

Wilson, E., *Islamic Designs*, British Museum Publications, London 1988

MAGAZINES

The following articles appeared in *India Magazine*, New Delhi:

Chhabra, T., 'Journey to Nyoolzu: A Toda Migration', February 1995

D'Gama Rose, R., 'A Journey in the Labyrithine Pols of Ahmedabad', August 1983

Engel, P., 'Jai Singh's Observatories', May 1992

Ganju, A., 'Desert Dwellings', December 1983

Gupta, S., 'Ancestral Mansions of the Peshwas. Poona', May 1987

Mohan, L., 'A Mansion for Kings in Vishnu's Abode', August 1984

Parihar, S., 'Mediaeval Caravansarais', May 1983

Patel, K., 'Chabutras', November 1988

Sampath Kumar, T. 'Bitodas', November 1984

Subhashini, A. V., 'Tharavads – Kerala's Nair Houses', July 1987

Thiagarajan, D., 'Ancestoral Abodes of Chettinad', February 1986

The following articles appeared in *Inside Outside*, Bombay:

Doctor, G., 'Dramatic Dimensions', August 1983

Doshi, B. V., 'The Vohrawads of Gujarat', August 1988

Parihar, S., 'Ancient Splendour', April 1989

Pinto, R., 'Cabo Raj Niwas', August 1988

Ramchandani, R., 'If there be a Paradise… Mughal Gardens', August 1988

GLOSSARY

attu loft

baithak sitting room
bajra millet
baluster small post or pillar, circular in section
bangla arched sloping roof (lit. 'from Bengal')
baraat groom's marriage party
bhandar treasury or store-room

caravansarai, caravanserai inn with large inner court
chabutra pigeon loft
chaitya ridged arch
chauk courtyard
chaukband built around a courtyard
charpoy bed with wooden frame
chejara mason
chhajja eaves, sunshade
chhatri domed pavilion supported by pillars
choki storeroom
chowkidar watchman
chorten pile of stones; memorial for holy man
chulha stove

dalan open-fronted chamber
daramshala see **caravansarai**
daulatkhana treasury
deodar Indian cypress
deshi see **swadeshi**
diwan-i-aam public reception room
diwan-i-khas private reception room
diwankhana formal reception room

firenghi foreign

garbha griha sanctuary, private place
ghats steps (esp. into pool or river); scarp slopes
gopura gateway

haveli mansion
illam homestead

jali latticework
jharoka covered balcony
jhinki marble powder
johara water tank

kachha unfinished, vernacular (lit. raw, unripe)
kani hall
khinp broom-like plant
kothi grain store
koond rainwater store
kuncha elephant grass

laterite type of red, iron-rich clay
loi fine plaster of ground brick and lime
lingam phallus, esp. for shrine

madhya griha inner court
mandapa hall for worshippers
mantrasala hall of audience
mardana men's area
mehrab niche
mistry mason
mod hamlet

obari grain store
otla, otlo open sitting platform

paniaru water store
parsal eating room
patara wheeled chest
patta planks
pilaster column or pillar, rectangular in section
pinjara kari elaborate form of **jali**
pisé compacted clay and stones
pol area of housing
potsherds fragments of pottery
pukka solidly built, permanent (lit. cooked)
punkah fan

puja prayer, religious ceremony
purlin horizontal roof beam

qibla direction of prayer for Muslims (towards Mecca)

rath covered bullock cart
ratha shrine

saag teak
saal bamboo
sarai see **caravansarai**
Shastra sacred Hindu writings
sikhara spire above temple sanctuary
sthpathi builder, architect
stupa reliquary monument
swadeshi indigenous, local

tankhu rainwater cistern
tarawad ancestral home
thabsang family room
tibari arched chamber
toda bracket
tolla door frame
trabeate constructed with horizontal beams

urch granary

vastu purusha male spirit that resides in building plot
vavdan windcatch
videshi foreign
vimana pyramidal tower

wada mansion; area of town

ziggurat stepped pyramid
zoondab enclosed balcony
zenana area reserved for women

189

Acknowledgments

While researching this book I travelled across almost every state in India. Firstly, my thanks are due to all those people throughout the country who showed me around their houses and patiently explained how and why things are done just so.

I am particularly indebted to Abubakr V. C. of Tellicherry and his family, especially Rashid C. P., Dr B. Allchin, Amita Baig, Peter Burman, Diana Campbell, Nand Kishor and Sulochana Choudhary of Killa Pardi, Sir Bernard Feilden, Kai Friese, Ashish Ganju, Aruna Ghose, John Gillow, Lakshmikant Jangid, Adil Jussawalla, Hershad Kumari, Bharat and Uma Patadia, John Pickford, Girish Chandra Sharma of Churu and family, especially Ravindra, Mary Spencer Watson, Jaidev and Nita Thakore, Nalini Thakur, Deborah Thiagaraja, Professor Kurula Varkay and Amrit and Goodie Vohra. Thanks also to Rabu Sharma for checking the text.

I am grateful to the India Office Library in London and the libraries of the School of Oriental and African Studies, London, Rurki University Engineering College, INTACH, New Delhi, School of Architecture and Planning, New Delhi, School of Architecture, Ahmedabad. Several collections of building types proved very useful, including Dakshinachitra near Madras, Indira Gandhi Rashtriya Manav Sangrahaliya, Bhopal and Shilpgram, Udaipur.

Ilay Cooper

Firstly, a special thank you to Lynne and Eric Baxendale. Many others, in several countries, have helped me in the preparation of this book.

In England: Kevin Gabbitas, H. A. West, Manchester; Andrew Vaines, Bradford; Nicola, Jenny and Joseph Dawson, Bradford; Fuji Film UK Ltd; Ian Taylor, Hull; John Gillow, Cambridge.

In Germany: Sibylle Hinterwinkler, Frankfurt.

In India: Chote and Pappu Kapoor and family, Jaipur; Vinnay and Anju, Niros Restaurant, Jaipur; Yadavendra and Arpana Singh, Samode Palace, Rajasthan; Punkaj and Mohan Singh, Amritsar; Hotel Airlines, Amritsar; C. P. Simon, Kerala; Klaus Schlizeineer, Kerala; Hotel Surya Samudra, Kerala; Len Hallegua, Kerala; N. D. and Renu Mehra and family, New Delhi; B. Mohana Chandran, Tamil Nadu; Mrs Deborah Thiagaraja, Tamil Nadu; and Dakshinachitra, Tamil Nadu.

Barry Dawson

Sources of Illustrations

Photographs by Barry Dawson:

3 (title page), 6–7, 23 (centre and right), 25, 26, 27 (above), 30, 34, 36, 37, 49 (left), 62, 63, 67, 68–69, 71 (below), 80–81, 82, 83, 84, 85, 87, 88, 91, 92, 93, 94, 95, 98 (above), 99, 100, 102, 107, 108–9, 109 (right and below), 115, 118, 119, 120, 122, 123, 125, 131, 132, 138–39, 142, 143, 144, 146–47, 148, 150 (below), 151, 152, 153, 154, 155 (above), 157, 158, 160, 161, 165, 166, 167, 170, 171, 172, 174, 175 (above), 178, 179

Photographs by Ilay Cooper:

2 (opposite title page), 22, 23 (left), 24, 27 (below), 31, 35, 38, 39, 42, 43, 45, 46–47, 49 (right), 50 (above), 53, 58, 59, 64, 66, 69 (above), 70, 71, 73, 76, 77, 86, 89, 96–97, 98 (below), 101, 104, 106, 108 (left), 111, 112, 113, 126, 127, 128, 134, 135, 150 (above), 155 (below), 156, 162–63, 164, 173 (below), 175 (below)

Drawings by Bryan Sentance:

25, 28, 29, 32, 33, 37, 48, 52, 53, 56, 57, 78, 82, 90, 95, 102, 107, 113, 121, 124, 130, 133, 141, 145, 165, 172, 177, 180, 181

Photographs by Ian Taylor:

50–51 (below), 51 (above), 52, 54, 55

190

INDEX